Decorating Details

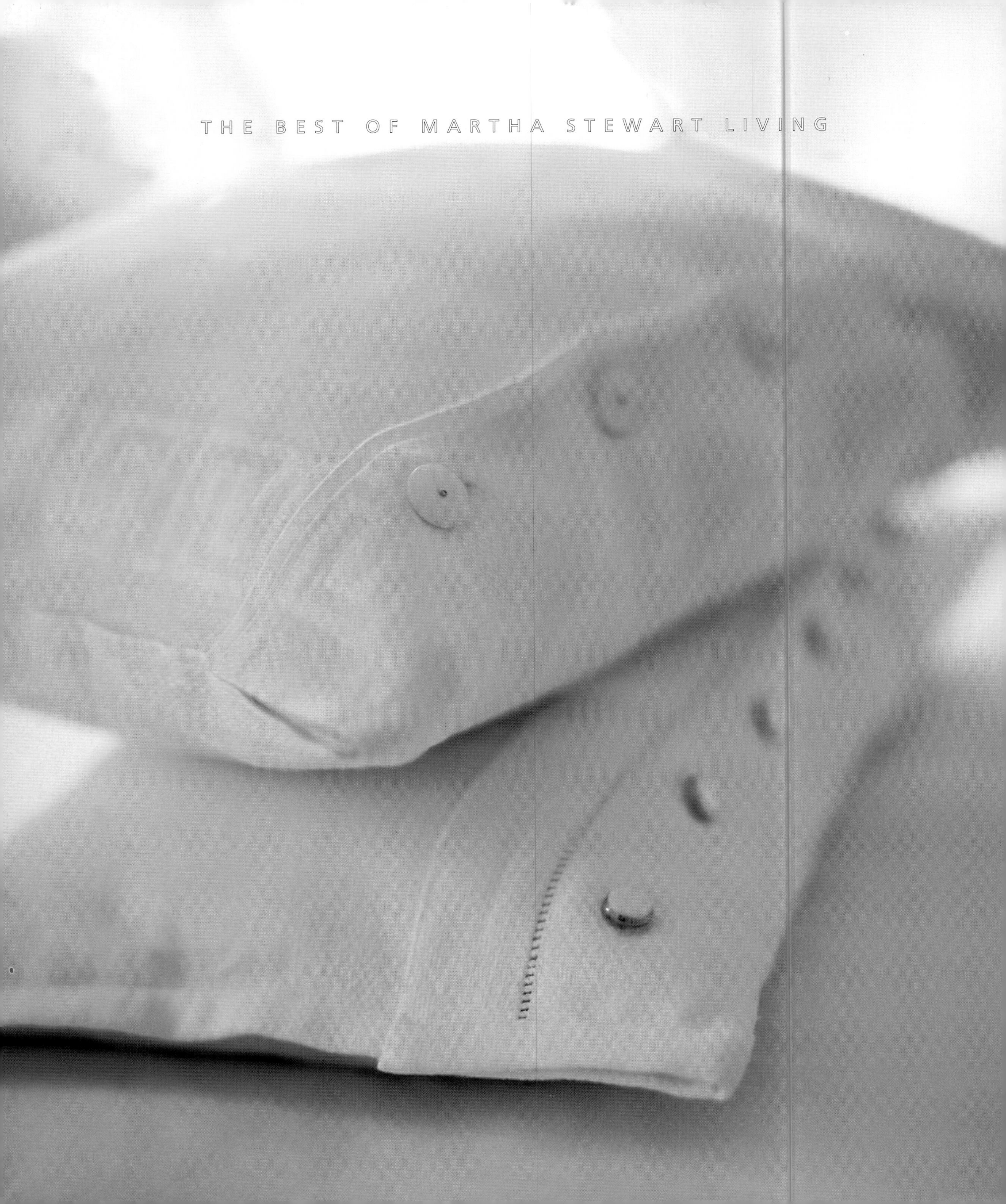
THE BEST OF MARTHA STEWART LIVING

Decorating Details

PROJECTS AND IDEAS FOR A MORE COMFORTABLE, MORE BEAUTIFUL HOME

Clarkson Potter/Publishers
New York

Thanks to the many photographers, editors,
art directors, stylists, and writers whose
inspirational ideas contributed to this volume.
And thanks to the entire staff of Martha
Stewart Living Omnimedia and to everyone
at Oxmoor House, Clarkson Potter, Satellite
Graphics, and Quebecor Printing whose
invaluable work helped produce this book.

Originally published in book form by
Martha Stewart Living Omnimedia LLC in 1998.
Published simultaneously by Clarkson N. Potter, Inc.,
Oxmoor House, Inc., and Leisure Arts.

Most of the photographs in this work were
previously published in MARTHA STEWART LIVING.

Published by Clarkson N. Potter, Inc.,
201 East 50th Street, New York, NY 10022.
Member of the Crown Publishing Group.
Random House, Inc. New York, Toronto,
London, Sydney, Auckland
http://www.randomhouse.com/
Clarkson N. Potter, Potter, and colophon
are trademarks of Clarkson N. Potter, Inc.

Printed in the United States of America.

Library of Congress Cataloging-in-Publication Data
Stewart, Martha.
Decorating details : projects and ideas for
a more comfortable, more beautiful home :
the best of Martha Stewart living. — 1st ed.
p. cm.
Includes index.
ISBN 0-609-80258-5 (alk. paper)
1. Interior decoration — Themes, motives.
I. Martha Stewart living. II. Title
NK2115.S67 1998 747 — dc21 97–44131 CIP

10 9 8 7 6 5 4 3 2 1
First Edition

Editor: Bruce Shostak
Designer: Linda Kocur
Writer: Celia Barbour
Managing Editor: Kyle T. Blood

Contents

Introduction

A MOST EXTRAORDINARY THING HAS JUST HAPPENED, SOMETHING THAT IN YEARS PAST I WOULD never have dreamed would occur: I bought a furnished, decorated house, complete with linens, dishes, rugs, and even curtains. Heretofore every living space I've ever bought or rented has been an empty, unrestored, unrenovated place that I've been pleased to plan, tear apart, redo, paint, and decorate in my particular style, to my particular taste.

What I'm quickly discovering is that decorating from scratch, beginning with a raw interior, is more like being an artist than a decorator. Nothing is set in stone—everything can be altered or adapted to fit one's own personal style. In my new old house, which has already had at least one person's taste imposed on it in terms of design, colors, furnishings, and even what I call "tchotchkes," the task of making alterations to fit my taste and style is a challenge that I look forward to, but one that also slightly intimidates me. As I contemplate all the changes that should and can be made, I realize that what faces me is the same as what faces the professional interior designer every single working day: altering an existing living space to fit the present owner's tastes, desires, and requirements in a pleasing, aesthetic, and affordable manner.

Considered in this way, the task seems infinitely more doable. This book, the second decorating volume of our BEST OF MARTHA STEWART LIVING series (the first is *How to Decorate*), is meant to help. Once the larger elements of interior design are done—the jobs of choosing the basic color scheme, the upholstery fabrics, the furniture and furniture groupings, the lighting schemes, the window treatments, and the flooring—what remains is the details, or what I like to call the "fun stuff." Decorating the walls with mirrors and framed artwork, choosing lamps and lampshades, placing and arranging bookcases and then the contents of such shelving, and even choosing or designing bedding and pillows should all be interesting and enjoyable, and done at a pace that, when completed, allows one to emit a sigh of relief that the house is now really and truly a home.

Martha Stewart

P.S. I'll let you know how the new house turns out.

THIS PAGE An eclectic grouping of objects and images animates the wall above a sofa. The arrangement includes oil paintings, sketches, a cameo display, and a wall bracket, all united by a quiet palette. The lowest picture, a nineteenth-century etched portrait, hangs just inches above the sofa, visually linking the wall's composition with the room's furniture. OPPOSITE A collection of circa-1870 travel photographs ascends a staircase wall. They are hung from French rods, which are hooked to a bar that runs parallel to the ceiling; hangers for the pictures can be positioned anywhere.

Pictures

Bringing walls to life with skillful arrangements

of objects and images

ABOVE A large sketch looms over a small watercolor, visually anchoring it in place and counterbalancing the painted Swedish chair below. Large pictures usually retain their impact even when they're hung high on walls; smaller pictures need to be seen at more intimate distances. OPPOSITE On the narrow wall between two large windows, a single image might get lost. Gilt-framed eighteenth-century landscape prints with French mats hang end to end, creating a bold column that elegantly fills the space. The pattern made by their adjoining frames subtly echoes the window muntins. The antique slipper chair, covered in milk-white velvet, softens the strong vertical lines with its gentle curves.

THE PICTURES YOU HANG ON YOUR WALLS SHOULD BE THINGS YOU LIKE to look at every day. A pressed leaf, a family photo, or a print found at a flea market can bring as much genuine style and personality to an interior as any museum masterpiece.

Ordinary objects and images, however, usually need a bit of finessing before they can hold their own in an interior. Finding the right frame is the first step. A well-chosen frame dignifies its contents and allows even the humblest picture, from a vintage playing card to a child's drawing, to have more presence in a room. Although a good frame is a beautiful object in its own right, it should never overwhelm its contents. In color, period, or style, the frame should complement whatever it contains.

The arrangement of pictures has as much impact as the pictures themselves. One rule of thumb used to be that you should hang every-thing at eye level, centered about five-and-a-half feet above the floor. But while that approach works fine in an art gallery, it's often too impersonal for a house, where pictures should interact more intimately with their surroundings. Lowering a picture to waist height on the wall relates it to the furniture—a comfortable reading chair, a telephone table—and lets it be appreciated by anyone sitting there. When you wish to draw the eye upward to beautiful crown moldings or to accentuate the space above a doorway, elevating a picture can easily do the trick.

While something important deserves to hang alone, with enough blank wall space around it to let it shine, quieter drawings, photographs, and prints often work best in groups. They may be strung along a hallway or clustered above a sofa or fireplace. Together, they should create a rhythm or pattern that has a greater presence than each one would have individually. But the rules are few: The only logic that matters is the logic of the eye.

ABOVE A picture shelf makes neat work out of an assortment of Martha's family photographs. A cast-iron wreath, originally an architectural ornament, frames a photograph of her mother. At left, her father's image is surrounded by a wide silk-wrapped mat and a silver-leaf frame. A photograph of a teenage Martha with an obedient crow sits between the two. The two-inch-deep shelf, with a lip to keep pictures in place, is mounted to the wall at chair-rail height. Such shelves are a great idea for people who like to rearrange artwork frequently: Images can be shuffled and replaced without ever contending with unsightly nail holes. OPPOSITE, TOP LEFT A trio of small pictures offers a refreshing view to anyone working at this Swedish–style writing desk. Overhead, an antique map of the northeastern United States tilts forward for better viewing. TOP RIGHT Art imitates life in a country dining room, where a vintage butterfly print in a flea-market frame hangs above a real butterfly mounted in a shadow box lined with pale-blue silk. BOTTOM LEFT Photographs from Martha's 1996 trip to Egypt wind their way along a twisting hallway. Framed as a series and hung at the same height, they unfold like a travelogue. The 1795 chair is from France. BOTTOM RIGHT In the traditional place of honor above a mantel, an assortment of small pictures forms a perfect square, giving them the impact of a single large work. The uneven space between the frames is all part of a successful overall composition.

  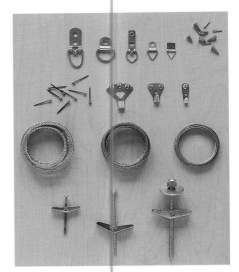

The best hardware to use when hanging a picture depends on the quality and composition of the wall, as well as the weight of the picture itself. If your walls are surfaced with beautiful plaster, wallpaper, or wood paneling, you will probably want to preserve them in the best condition possible. And if you move or replace pictures frequently, you need an option that doesn't leave a permanent mark behind. That means suspending pictures from something other than a nail or screw inserted directly into the wall. Picture molding, common in traditional houses, offers a practical alternative. A variety of S-hooks (above left) are designed to hang from the molding. Since both the hook and the cord or wire are visible, choose them carefully. A variety of vintage S-hooks can be found at flea markets and antiques stores. Silk or cotton cords, metal chains, or ribbons can all be used to suspend the picture.

Another option is using French rods (above center), common in art galleries. A horizontal bar is installed near the ceiling. Metal rods hook over a lip on the bar; they are fitted with one or more hooks that slide up and down the rods, so you can place pictures precisely.

If you prefer to keep hardware out of sight, you'll need to make holes in the wall behind the picture. First, find out what your walls are made of. Drywall is a factory-made panel of gypsum plaster sandwiched between layers of paper; it's installed on a support of vertical two-by-fours, called studs, generally spaced 16" on center. Plaster, common in houses built before 1945, is troweled over a skeleton of wooden lath.

Light- to medium-weight pictures can be hung from picture hooks (above right, second row from top) nailed directly into either type of wall. For heavier pictures, it's wise to figure out where a stud is located behind drywall, and insert the nail into the stud. Or you can use a toggle bolt (above right, bottom row), which has a pair of arms that fold flat against the bolt when you insert it into the wall, then flare out behind the drywall panel when the screw is tightened. Fragile plaster may be best served by a molly bolt, a machine screw with a sleeve; insert the sleeve into a predrilled hole, then tighten the screw in the sleeve.

The most stable way to hang pictures is to attach a D-ring (above right, top row) to each side of the frame, then slip each one over a picture hook mounted to the wall. This method keeps pictures from tilting or wobbling, but does require precise measuring, since no final adjustments can be made once the picture is up. If you prefer picture wire (above right, third row), measure a length that's eight inches longer than the width of the frame. Thread it through the D-rings, and pull four inches of wire through either side; fold the short end back, and twist it tightly around the main wire several times. Hang picture wire on a picture hook.

PLANNING AN ARRANGEMENT

Before putting a single hole in the wall, establish the arrangement of pictures and pieces (top). In front of the wall where you plan to hang the objects, lay them out on the floor and lean them up against the wall or a piece of furniture; move them until the results suit you. For an eclectic grouping like the one on page 10, the spacing doesn't need to be even, but try to avoid "rivers" of space running horizontally or vertically between pictures. Measure the height and width of the entire grouping to be sure that it will fit into the space allotted. When you are ready to hang, begin with a central picture or object, and work outward from there. A carpenter's level (above) is an indispensable tool. If you are using two D-rings to hang a picture, mark two spots on the wall for the hardware, and use the level to be sure they're even, adjusting as necessary before putting hardware in the wall. If you are using one picture hook and wire on the back of the frame, hang the picture, then use the level to straighten it.

TILTING A PICTURE

When a mirror or piece of art cants forward from a wall, it offers dimension to the room and a new perspective on the piece itself. The map on page 15 and the bird print on page 23 are actually hung from picture hooks in the wall, with picture wire strung between two D-rings on the back of the frame; this is more secure than hanging it from the molding. The roping above the map (below) is purely decorative; it extends from the frame to a vintage picture hanger on the molding. To hang the piece securely at an angle, position D-rings lower than normal on the back of the frame (not quite halfway down the frame; measure to make sure they're even). Secure a length of picture wire between D-rings, leaving some slack. Install two picture hooks on the wall, using a level to make sure that they are straight. Then hang the picture. Elevate the bottom edge of frame until the top leans forward at the angle you want; using a pencil, mark where the bottom of the frame touches the wall, about 1" in from each side. Remove the picture. Hammer two small nails into the wall at the markings until the nail heads protrude about ¼" from the wall. Hang the picture, and rest the bottom edge on the nails. As a safety measure, press the picture hooks shut around the picture wire. Paint nail heads the color of the wall.

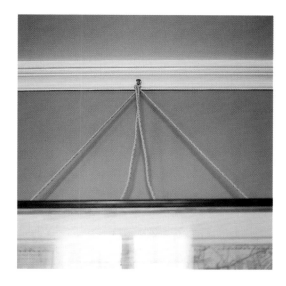

OPPOSITE A family album is splashed across the wall of a study. Two decades' worth of favorite pictures are united by inexpensive eight-by-ten-inch frames, oriented horizontally or vertically to suit the images. The frames are available in natural or pickled wood; some were painted white for contrast. THIS PAGE A collection of sepia horticultural prints forms an orderly grid that fills the bare wall above a Regency-style bench in a foyer. Such a high-impact arrangement can be taken in at a glance; it works well in transitional areas like this one, where people frequently pass through.

ABOVE Arranged above and below a strong horizontal center line, an assortment of twentieth-century photographs forms a striking pattern on a sitting-room wall. The simple wooden frames, stained coffee and black, play up the warm sepia tones of the black-and-white photographs. The mats vary in width; the widest ones appear to isolate the images within. All the mats are slightly deeper at the bottom than at the top, a classic rule of picture framing that makes the image appear to be centered in the frame. A white nesting table from the thirties sits at the head of a French mahogany daybed, upholstered in mattress ticking.

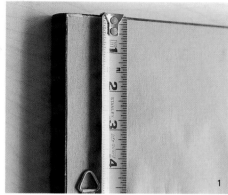

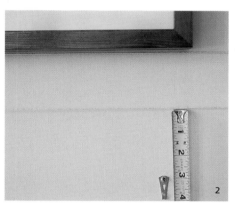

ALIGNING A ROW OF PICTURES

To create the horizontally aligned arrangement shown opposite and above, stretch two pieces of string taut between pushpins to create a guide for even spacing. When an arrangement covers a long stretch of wall space, as it does here, insert a pushpin every three or four feet to keep the string from sagging. A D-ring screwed into each side of a frame makes for the most secure and precise picture hanging. Don't estimate measurements; always use a tape measure. 1 For the bottom row of pictures, measure the distance from the top of a frame to the top of the D-ring. 2 Make the distance from the string to the bottom of the picture hook the same (remember that the nail should be inserted in the wall ½" or more above this point, depending on the size of the hook); repeat process for all pictures on the bottom row. For the top row of pictures, measure the

distance from the bottom of a frame to the top of the D-ring, and match that to the distance from the upper string to the bottom of the picture hook. Although these pictures vary dramatically in size, they are actually paired quite carefully according to width: Each one above the line is approximately the same width as the one below it. Where there are differences, each pair of pictures is centered vertically, rather than aligned along the right or left sides of the frames. This pushpin-and-string technique is especially useful for hanging pictures along a staircase: Above the bottom step, mark a spot on the wall where you want the bottom of a picture to be. Measure this distance, and mark the same distance above the top step. Run a length of string between these two points, and hang pictures so that the lower right- or left-hand corners meet the string.

OPPOSITE A Victorian watercolor of a morning glory is suspended from the front of a bookcase. Most shelves are part furniture and part wall; placing a picture on the surface emphasizes the former characteristic. Other objects on the shelves, including Venetian glassware, art pottery, and small standing pictures, vary the rhythm of the arrangement. ABOVE An 1860s English mirror frame by Watts drops from picture molding to hang over a nineteenth-century English side chair. A coral satin ribbon covers the wire securing it in place. ABOVE RIGHT On a guest-bedroom door, a simple frame made of barn siding holds an old playing card sandwiched between two panes of glass. Grosgrain ribbon threaded through two holes drilled in the top of the frame hangs the picture. RIGHT A bird takes flight above a doorway, a perfect spot for a visual surprise; in China, the space over a door has long been considered an auspicious place for art.

ABOVE LEFT Four very simple, inexpensive frames mounted together create an impressive home for an evocative quartet of photographs. The frames have flat edges, so they can be joined flush, and gentle beveled fronts that create an interesting play of light and shadows. They are painted two contrasting shades of bluish gray, chosen to complement the color of the walls. A velvet ribbon suspends the pictures from a vintage picture nail head. ABOVE RIGHT A trio of wedding photographs unfolds from the wall. Painted three shades of stone gray, the frames contain a progression of moments from a memorable day.

HOW TO MAKE A QUADRANT FRAME

Favorite old photographs take on a new look when viewed together in a quadrant (opposite, left; that's Martha's daughter, Alexis, at age 1½ in the upper-right-hand frame). To make the quadrant, you'll need four 3"-by-5" unfinished pine frames; primer; matte or semigloss paint; six mounting brackets with screws; and two D-rings. Vintage picture nails can be found at flea markets and antiques stores. 1 Prime the unfinished frames, and let them dry. Sand lightly, and apply two coats of paint, allowing paint to dry between coats. The two colors chosen here are slightly paler than the color of the wall; each color was used for the two frames that are diagonally opposite from each other. Once the paint has dried, after about 4 hours, position the frames as you want them to appear on the wall. 2 Turn them face down, and join them with the mounting brackets. Insert the glass, photographs, and backing material; close according to manufacturer's instructions. Screw the two D-rings to the back top corners. Select a velvet ribbon in a complementary color, and run it through the D-rings. Hang the finished piece from a vintage picture nail in the wall above.

HOW TO MAKE A TRIPTYCH

This three-picture frame helps you re-create your favorite memories in a sequence. You'll need three 3"-by-5" unfinished pine frames, four hinges with screws, paint, and cardstock. Make sure the frames have straight edges, so they'll open flat against the wall. Prime, lightly sand, and paint the frames with two coats of paint. (These are all painted the same color, but you could just as well paint them three contrasting colors.) 1 Once the paint has dried, connect two frames with a pair of hinges, mounting the hinges with the pivots facing out. Connect the third frame to the other two with the remaining pair of hinges. Place the glass, photographs, and backing material in the frames, and close according to the manufacturer's instructions. If your photographs are too large, don't cut them. Instead, have a photo lab reproduce images to size—either from the original negatives or from the photos themselves. 2 Cut three pieces of neutral-colored cardstock to the size of the backing, and attach to the backs with glazier's points. Attach two D-rings to each side of the middle frame; measure to make sure they're even. Hang the triptych on two nails, or on two wall screws for extra support.

OPPOSITE A selection of nineteenth- and twentieth-century spools and bobbins is displayed in a shadow box constructed behind a flea-market frame. The back panel is made of a piece of foam board covered with linen; the spools are held in place by thread sewn through the panel. Cherished objects that you collect, like these, or those that you inherit or simply find on the beach need not sit neglected in drawers. Displayed in shadow boxes, they become works of art for your walls. ABOVE LEFT Insect specimens float inside simple shadow boxes. Poised between two pieces of glass, the insects cast unusual shadows on the wall behind them. ABOVE RIGHT A shadow box purchased from an art-supply store has been personalized to house a beachcomber's treasures. Panels of driftwood line the back of the box, while a vintage print of two fish has been glued on top. The starfish and anemones are balanced between the front and back panels of the box. This is the easiest of the three projects shown on these pages, as it requires no hammering or mitering, just gluing.

  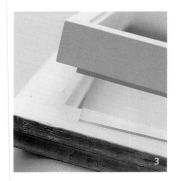 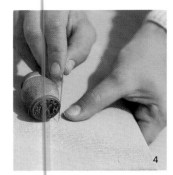

HOW TO MAKE A PICTURE-FRAME SHADOW BOX

To make the shadow box shown on page 26, you'll need a new or antique picture frame (the rabbet, the recessed area that normally holds the glass, artwork, and backing, must be at least ½" deep); 1"-by-2" pine board; ¼"-by-2" lattice; foam board; ⅛" Plexiglas cut to fit the frame; ⅛" wooden shims; four-penny nails; double-sided tape; wood glue; four right-angle clamps; four spring clamps; hammer; linen; needle and thread; four mending brackets; and hanging hardware. For this shadow box, the 2" width of both the pine boards and the lattice determines its depth; if the objects you wish to showcase require a deeper space, have a lumberyard cut the boards and rip lattice to fit. Place the frame face down on a flat surface, and measure the width of the opening; cut two pieces of pine board to match. Measure the length of the frame's opening, add 1½", and cut two pieces of board to this length. 1 Glue the four boards together at the corners to form a box; use the right-angle clamps to hold pieces together. Let dry 30 minutes. Secure corners with two four-penny nails, and lightly sand all edges. The box should fit squarely over the opening in the back of the frame. 2 Place four shims in the corners of the rabbet to represent the thickness of the Plexiglas, and position frame face down on a work surface. Align the box on top of the frame. Measure the inside length of the box, and cut two pieces of lattice to match. Then measure the inside width, subtract ½", and cut two pieces to this dimension. With the box on top of the frame, position the lattice strips, which will act as spacers, so they protrude into the rabbet and abut the wooden shims. You will notice a recessed space where the shadow box will meet the wall; this is where the backing will lie. Glue the lattice spacers to the inside of the box, using the spring clamps to keep in place. Let dry 30 minutes. Remove the box and spacers from the frame. Prime all surfaces, let dry, and sand lightly. Paint back of frame and box with two coats of paint, allowing to dry between coats. 3 Position the Plexiglas in the frame. Apply glue around the perimeter of the opening, and set the box on top. Rest a weighted board on top of the box until glue dries, about 30 minutes, wiping off any excess glue. Cut the foam board to fit the recessed area in the box. Cut the linen to cover the board, adding 2" to each side, and iron the linen. Center foam board on linen. Trim excess fabric by cutting triangles of linen away ⅛" from corners. Lay a strip of double-edged tape along back edge of foam board. Pull linen over edge of that side, and press to tape. Repeat on opposite side, making sure fabric tension is uniform. Attach linen on other two sides, using a bone folder or knife tip to tuck in excess corners. 4 Arrange the objects to be displayed on the linen-covered foam board, and sew them into place with heavy neutral-colored thread. Secure board with objects to back of the shadow box with 1½" mending brackets, screwed into the wood. Attach two screw eyes to the back of original frame, and string picture wire between. Hang shadow box on the wall with appropriate picture hook.

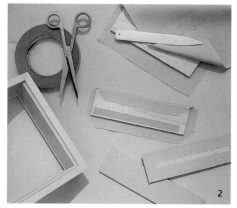

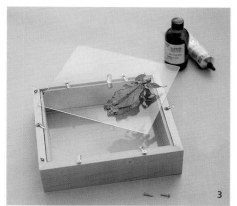

HOW TO MAKE A GLASS SHADOW BOX

To make both the 7"-by-11" and 8"-by-11" shadow boxes shown on page 27, you'll need to buy the lumber precut from a framer. Explain that you're making shadow boxes, and ask to have ¾" maple frame stock cut with mitered ends to the following dimensions: four 8" pieces, two 7" pieces, and two 11" pieces. In addition to the maple, you'll also need: ¼" balsa wood; four pieces of ⅛" Plexiglas cut to size; two pieces of ½"-long Plexiglas rod; methylene chloride adhesive; wood glue; double-sided tape; eight right-angle clamps; linen; and twelve ¾" turn pins. Make the smaller box first. 1 Glue together one 8" piece of maple and one 7" piece; hold together with a right-angle clamp until glue has set. Repeat with two other pieces, and then glue all four pieces together. 2 Measure the inside surfaces of the frame; cut four balsa-wood spacers to fit, subtracting ¼" from the width to accommodate the two sheets of Plexiglas. Cut four pieces of linen to cover the spacers, adding 1" of fabric on all sides. Center a spacer on the linen. Cut triangles of fabric, ⅛" from the corners of the balsa. Lay a strip of double-sided tape along the back edge of the spacer. Pull the linen over, and press it onto the tape to secure, making sure that the tension of the fabric is uniform across the surface. Use a bone folder to tuck in excess fabric at corners. Repeat for the other three spacers. 3 Glue spacers to insides of box; let dry. Place one piece of Plexiglas in frame. Place a small drop of adhesive on center of other Plexiglas and another drop on end of rod. Let set a moment, then add another drop to each surface. Stick rod to glass; let glue dry. Place a drop of adhesive on other end of rod; place insect on top; let dry. Fit Plexiglas into back of frame so it rests on spacer. Secure with six turn pins; add screw eyes at top corners; use ribbon or cord to hang. Repeat steps 1 through 3 with remaining material for larger frame.

THIS PAGE A mix of small tables and stools brings flexibility to living-room arrangements: A thrift-store ottoman reupholstered in chenille and fitted with casters serves as a cocktail table; the small footstool underneath can slide out to provide a surface for a plate of hors d'oeuvres. OPPOSITE A vintage wooden box transformed into a small footstool holds keepsakes that otherwise might clutter the modern glass coffee table above it.

Tables & Stools

Transforming forgotten furniture into stylish, versatile pieces

TABLES AND STOOLS ARE THE SIMPLEST OF HOME FURNISHINGS, MERELY surfaces on legs. But you cannot create a room without them. Tables help to organize a room's activities. A coffee table makes an arrangement of chairs more sociable; without it, they'd be gathered around empty space, as aimlessly as in a waiting room. End tables support lamps and teacups, allowing you to read and sip. A bedside table allows you to keep books, light, water, and an alarm by your side. Stools are even more versatile. A plush ottoman can double as a table when a tray is placed on top. A pair of tall stools can flank a bed or stand side by side as a two-part coffee table. A stool can also be a seat, footrest, or pedestal.

The placement of tables is usually dictated by need: Wherever people might sit or lie, there should be a table close at hand. The arrangement of stools can be more serendipitous. Like cats and children, stools can make themselves at home in the unlikeliest spots, cozying up behind a sofa, or converting the void beneath a table into a small furnished room.

Although tabletops are often used as elbow rests or footrests, their main job is to hold things, not bodies. But too many objects can overwhelm any surface. A few carefully chosen items have the most impact, and they allow your table or stool to serve its role with grace as well as utility.

A wide variety of tables and stools—from prairie-size coffee tables to lily-pad-size footstools—is available at antiques stores and tag sales. Many will seem dated or hopelessly worn at first glance. But because these pieces are so basic, they're easy to revamp. Before refurbishing a table or stool, though, consider how you want to use it. A hard-topped kitchen stool can become a comfortable seat with the addition of a pillow, and an upholstered footrest can become a stereo stand if the padding is replaced with a glass top. On the following pages you'll find ideas for many transformations.

HOW TO MAKE A COFFEE-TABLE OTTOMAN

The chenille-covered ottoman on page 30 was only a few decades old when it was discovered at a flea market, so it was in pretty good shape. But the padding was squishy and the proportions uninspired. We gave it more elegant dimensions by lengthening the legs with a set of brass socket casters. For the best fit, the caster should be just a bit narrower than the leg. To install a caster: 1 Mark the leg with tape where the top of the caster will be, and use a rasp to shave down the wood. Mount the caster, and repeat with the other legs. 2 Hammer brass nails with decorative heads along bottom edge of the ottoman. A professional upholsterer gave this ottoman a taut new cover. Reupholstering at home isn't easy, but it can be done. First, remove the original fabric. Measure the size of the ottoman's top. Add the height plus 3" to all sides, and cut fabric to this dimension. Center the fabric right-side down on the ottoman, and mark the four corners with tailor's chalk. Lay the fabric flat, then square the corners as follows: Fold a corner on the diagonal with right sides facing, so the raw edges meet. Draw a straight line from the chalk mark perpendicular to the raw edge; sew a seam along this line. Repeat for the other four corners. Trim excess fabric. Turn right-side out, and press. Cut a piece of batting to fit the ottoman's top. Place the batting on the ottoman; slip the cover over it. Turn the ottoman upside down, and pull the fabric to the underside. Carefully cut away fabric around the legs, and staple underneath. Cut a piece of black upholstery backing to the dimensions of the underside of the stool. Fold under ½" on all sides, and press flat. Tack in place.

An old wooden box is easily transformed into the footstool shown on page 31. Any simple lidded box, like an old shoeshine box, would work well. To raise the box off the ground, create four ball feet by sawing unfinished drapery-rod finials off at the neck. Sand, prime, and paint both the inside and outside of the box. Prime and paint the feet the same color. Attach the feet with screws from the inside of the box. Fasten nickel-plated bin handles to two sides of the box. 1 For the upholstered top, cut a piece of linen just bigger than the size you want the padded area to be, and cut a piece of bonded Dacron batting just smaller than the linen. Fold and press the linen edges under. Center the batting on the box, and place the linen over it. Staple the two materials to the box at all four corners and once or twice along each side. Cover each edge with a length of grosgrain ribbon. Insert upholstery tacks every inch, tapping them in with a tack hammer. To give shiny heads a matte finish, brush with steel wool before hammering. 2 Store photo albums, stationery, books—or anything you might want on hand while relaxing on the sofa—in the storage stool.

HOW TO MAKE A LINEN-TOPPED STOOL

A simple renovation updates the pair of French stools on page 33 while protecting their original oxblood paint. Their wooden tops aren't fine wood; they are meant to be upholstered. Stretch linen across the top, and staple the edges on the sides. Attach grosgrain ribbon with craft glue over the staples. Buy a pillow insert the same dimensions as the stool's top. To make the fringed pillowcase, measure the dimensions of the pillow; add ½" to all sides. Cut two pieces of linen to these dimensions. Measure the perimeter of the pillow; add 1", and cut a piece of moss fringe to this length. Pin the strip of fringe to the perimeter of one linen square, with the fringe facing inward and the edges aligned. Sew around the perimeter, ½" in from the edge. Align the second fabric square over the first so that fringe is sandwiched between them. Sew around three sides, ½" from edge. Turn case right-side out; press seam. Insert pillow, and slip-stitch closed.

HOW TO CUSHION A METAL-FRAME STOOL

The taller striped stool on page 37 has a thin metal frame. Smooth any rough spots by lightly sanding the surface, giving the finish "tooth" for the primer to adhere (if the piece is very smooth, use steel wool). Wipe clean with a damp cloth. Prime the frame, and let dry. Apply two coats of paint, sanding between coats. Cut a piece of ½"-thick plywood to fit inside the metal frame; cover the board with fabric (stripes tend to be a bit challenging to align), and attach with staples to the underside. To make the cushion insert, cut 2"-thick foam and a piece of batting to the dimensions of the top. Measure the perimeter of the top; add 2". To this length, cut a 3"-wide strip of fabric for the side of the case and a 1½"-wide strip for the piping. To make the piping, wrap the narrower strip right-side out around a length of ¼" cotton cording with raw edges even; secure with pins as you go. Stitch along the fabric to encase the cord, leaving a ½" seam allowance. Pin the piping to the right side of the wider strip, with the cord facing inward and the raw edges flush. Stitch in place, following the seam line in the piping. Cut two squares of fabric to the dimension of the stool's top plus ½" on all sides. Pin piping around the perimeter of one square, right sides facing and raw edges flush. Clip seam at corners to keep flat; sew together. Pin second square to the other edge of strip, right sides inward. Sew together around three sides, clipping the seams at the corners. Turn right-side out, and insert the foam square. Slip-stitch closed, and place on stool.

OPPOSITE TOP A sturdy coffee table was made by cutting down the legs of a 1910 kitchen table, painting it white, and fitting it with a galvanized-steel top. Its broad proportions and informal style suit this cottage's spacious living room. Because coffee tables have been around for less than a hundred years, they can be difficult to find in period styles. Reworking an older table type, as done here, often offers the best solution. The chairs are oak office furniture from a flea market, painted white to match the table. OPPOSITE BOTTOM A fifties diner-style coffee cup sits on a coffee table topped with milk glass, cut to fit and polished smooth at the edges. ABOVE LEFT A vintage wooden kitchen table shortened into a coffee table and covered with a $^3/_8$-inch-thick glass top is sleek and easy to clean. A large porcelain serving dish holds a collection of black-and-white photographs. Rather than permanently displaying an array of objects, the tabletop is left almost bare, so it can shift quickly from being a surface for games or reading to an informal dining table when friends drop by. Items for display—ironstone pitchers and gravy boats—perch upon the vintage plant stand nearby. ABOVE RIGHT Matching paint and fabric unify two different stools. The taller one started out as a plain black metal frame, most likely the base for a tile- or stone-topped table. With a thin cushion, it becomes soft enough to be a seat and firm enough to hold a coffee cup on a saucer. The smaller of the two, with its boldly turned legs, is a William and Mary revival footstool.

OPPOSITE In a small, densely furnished living room, the role of the coffee table is played by a stool that once belonged to a vanity table. The stool's thinly padded top has been reupholstered in linen, and its slender turned legs are painted white so that they all but disappear against the painted floor. This light, simple stool marks the visual and emotional center of the room without overwhelming the space, the way a massive coffee table would. Along the far wall, a substantial oak tavern table, circa 1700, supports a lamp made from an ornate marble finial. The reproduction cloverleaf candle stand in the corner brings an element of verticality to the room's arrangement, reiterated by the silver candlestick and *Phalaenopsis* orchid on top. The sofa, covered in mattress ticking, is dressed up with silk-satin pillows. A slipper chair and an English Regency–style armchair flank the entrance. ABOVE The main room in a summer cottage is a gathering space for friends by day and a guest room by night. A wrought-iron bench with a top made from woven rope serves as a coffee table; a sycamore tray gives it a solid surface. The bench doubles as a suitcase stand. The contemporary silver-leafed daybed is covered in celery-green linen, and an assortment of linen-covered pillows and bolsters (see pages 126 and 127 for how to make them) are arranged on top. The gateleg table in the corner is from the twenties.

LEFT At Martha's East Hampton home, a cast-iron garden table comes into the parlor to serve as a coffee table. Martha found the piece at a junk shop, scraped and painted the frame, and had a glass top cut to fit. Despite its substantial weight, the table appears almost airy, due to its transparent surface and cream-colored legs. The nineteenth-century Eastlake–style occasional table next to the doors displays garden roses in a blown-glass urn, whose mate is on the mantel. The chairs are covered with glazed linen in both plain and damask weaves. ABOVE On Martha's winter porch, a wrought-iron garden table is a fanciful focus in front of a garden sofa fitted with a set of new linen cushions. Cast-plaster antique heads rest upon the table's surface, which was cut from frosted glass.

ABOVE On an outdoor deck, a high proportion of tables to chairs accommodates a wide variety of activities, from Sunday morning newspaper reading to an evening party for twenty milling guests. Rustproof wire chairs from the fifties sit beside a pair of end tables topped with glass mosaic tiles. A Japanese split-bamboo mat is spread underfoot, visually dividing the space into distinct areas. In the background, an iron Empire–style chair painted green pulls up to a card table; the table's concretelike top is actually made from a lightweight, weatherproof mixture of plaster and resin. A pair of pillows makes the wooden bench more inviting. A potted evergreen, sitting atop a forties laboratory stool newly finished in metallic auto-body paint, can be rolled indoors in inclement weather.

HOW TO TILE A METAL-FRAME TABLE

Metal-frame tables from the sixties and seventies are widely available at flea markets and tag sales, with or without their original removable tops. These tables are virtually indestructible and equally at home indoors or out. A fresh coat of paint and a newly tiled surface will give one an air of quiet sophistication. To tile a table for use outdoors like the one shown on the opposite page, measure the tabletop dimensions. Subtract ¼" all around, and cut ⅜"-thick marine-grade plywood to this size. (You can also use a ¼"-thick piece of steel, which will make the table heavier but will last longer if left out in the rain over time; have a custom metal worker cut the steel to size and file the edges smooth.) Cut a sheet of glass mosaic tiles the same size as the plywood. To make a striped pattern as shown here, cut strips of different colored tiles,

and tape the tops of the strips together. Other patterns can be made by arranging individual tiles, face down, on a piece of clear adhesive shelf paper. 1 Mix epoxy according to package directions, then add just enough cement filler to create a thick paste. Using a trowel, spread a ⅛"-thick layer of paste onto the plywood. 2 Lay the sheet of tiles onto the paste, paper-side up. Press the tiles into the paste with a grouting float, a sponge for leveling grout; let tiles set for at least 24 hours, until they don't budge when prodded. 3 Moisten the paper backing with a sponge; wait 10 minutes. Pulling at a 45-degree angle, peel off the paper. 4 Next apply a layer of grout over the tiles with the grouting float, pressing grout down between the tiles. Leave as thin a film as possible. Allow the grout to set 20 minutes, then sponge grout off the surface of the tiles.

OPPOSITE A vanity stool placed under a nineteenth-century faux bamboo table in an entrance hall provides a place to sit and pull on boots or open the day's mail, and its festive color enlivens the room. A tiny African footstool on the tabletop supports a vase of flowers. To the right, a contemporary ceramic dish holds keys and change. The gilt mirror is Federal–style. ABOVE LEFT Before it was refurbished, this American Empire footstool was dark and hulking. It was also in shabby condition: The wood veneer was chipped and the velvet upholstery worn. Patched with wood putty and painted white, its clean, animated shape becomes more whimsical than grave. And a glass top makes it a sleek and practical stereo stand. The $1/2$-inch-thick green-glass top was cut to fit, then painted white on the underside to give it a milky effect. The chrome lamp and Art Deco club chair are both French. A pair of galvanized-steel boxes holds a collection of CDs. ABOVE RIGHT A humble mid-century stool painted white and upholstered in raffia becomes a light and summery addition to a hallway, filling an area where more substantial furniture wouldn't make sense. It displays an arrangement of tulips in a vintage opaque-blue glass vase.

HOW TO SEW A ROUND SLIPCOVER

The cotton-piqué slipcover on page 44 has teal piping to match the stool's legs. It makes a good project for experienced sewers. To begin, measure seat's top, and add ½" all around. Cut out a circle to this dimension. Measure the seat's height and circumference. Add ½" to all sides, and cut a strip to this dimension. Turn the seat over, and mark the center of the circle. Beginning at the center, measure back to the circle's edge, and add 1"; this is the length of the triangle's sides. Measure the arc between two stool legs; this is the base of the triangle. Add ½" to all dimensions, and cut eight triangles to fit. Sew pairs of triangles together along the straight sides, with right sides facing, to create four flaps. Turn right-side out, and press flat. Sew buttonholes in three of the flaps, beginning ½" in from the points. Sew a button onto the fourth, 1" from the point. Make piping as follows: Cut a piece of teal fabric on the bias into 1½"-wide strips. Sew strips end to end to make two lengths, each one 1" longer than the circumference of the circle. Wrap each strip right-side out, with raw edges aligned, around a length of ¼" cotton cording. Pin and sew the length of the strip. Trim to ½" from the seam. Pin and sew the piping to either long edge of the side strip, so that the piping faces inward and raw edges are aligned. Pin and sew the strip to the circumference of the circle, right sides facing, notching the seam allowance so the strip stays smooth. Pin and sew the four triangles to the other edge of the side, spacing them evenly around the circumference, and notching the seam allowance. Turn right-side out, and press. Wrap cover over the seat, and button the three flaps onto the fourth.

ENAMEL AND WAXED-LATEX FINISHES

All the white furniture pictured in this chapter was painted in one of two ways. Pieces with a hard, shiny finish, such as the stereo stand on page 45, were finished with enamel paint. Furniture with a softer look, such as the bedside table on page 47, received a coat of latex paint and was then buffed with wax. Enamel is more durable, best for furniture that gets heavy wear or is exposed to moisture, while a waxed latex finish looks more traditional. Regardless of the technique, prepare the piece this way: First, wash the surface thoroughly using a solution of ½ cup phosphate-free powdered cleaner in 1 gallon hot water, scrubbing gently with a sponge or a natural-bristle brush. Rinse, pat dry with a towel, and let dry overnight. Fill any cracks with wood filler, and let dry half an hour. Sand filled areas until flush with the surface, then sand the entire piece with medium-grade sandpaper (#100 for rough pieces, #150 for finer ones) to smooth any surface imperfections and to raise a "tooth" to which the primer bonds. Wipe with a tack cloth or damp rag. Now you're ready to paint. To create a waxed latex finish: Apply one coat of latex primer. Let dry. Apply two coats of flat latex, letting dry between coats. When thoroughly dry, rub a turpentine-based wax such as clear Briwax or Butcher's Wax lightly over the entire surface with a clean cotton rag or sponge. Wipe off any excess wax, wait 15 minutes, then buff lightly until a satiny shine comes through. For an enamel finish: Apply an all-purpose primer with a synthetic-bristle brush. Let dry 24 hours. Apply two to four coats of oil-based enamel in an eggshell finish; wait 24 hours between applications. For a higher shine, use a semigloss or high-gloss paint.

LEFT AND ABOVE LEFT In two corners of the same bedroom, mismatched tables are unified by white paint. The one by the chair is an inexpensive Victorian occasional table. The one by the bed is a lightweight pine pedestal from the thirties. The matching lamps are made from porch finials, and the patterned shade is made from forties wallpaper. The boudoir chair, also from the forties, is slipcovered in striped cotton, the same fabric used for the bed skirt.

ABOVE A Victorian cast-iron bed is surrounded by modern bentwood furnishings designed by Finnish architect Alvar Aalto in the thirties. The bedside table, one of a set of three nesting tables, holds bedtime comforts, including a glass decanter, a lamp with a resin globe shade, and a vase of eucalyptus; the stool tucked underneath provides a shelf for books and magazines. At the foot of the bed, a slatted bench holds a few extra blankets for chilly nights.

OPPOSITE An Italian iron vanity stool from the fifties is outfitted for the bathroom in a terry-cloth slipcover, making it the perfect place to sit and dry off after a shower, or to place an assortment of toiletries, contained on a ceramic tray. The slipcover with decorative tabs, made from a towel that matches the others in the bathroom, slides off for easy laundering. ABOVE LEFT A tall Victorian stool makes a fine bedside table, with a plum-colored slipcover tied in place to protect its original needlepoint cushion. A black tray provides a firm surface for a steel swing-arm reading lamp, a small clock, and an arrangement of sweet peas. Nearby, a squat Victorian boudoir stool, with its original tufted pink silk upholstery intact, makes a convenient step up onto the high iron bed, covered with a vintage cotton Marseilles spread. ABOVE RIGHT A tablecloth made by crisscrossing pale-green linen runners protects the surface of a newly painted bedside table without obscuring its shapely legs. A contemporary fiberglass desk lamp illuminates bedtime stories. A sterling-silver tumbler holds an arrangement of narcissi. The wind-up alarm clock is from the fifties. The rug is a contemporary wool kilim.

HOW TO MAKE A CORD-TIED SLIPCOVER

A cord-tied slipcover in plum-colored cotton protects the top of the antique stool on page 48. To make the cover, measure the length and width of the stool's top; add 4 inches to all sides. Cut a piece of fabric to this larger dimension; any upholstery-weight fabric will do. To make the rounded corners, find a lid or dessert plate that fits into the corner of the fabric, and trace the round edge onto the fabric. Repeat for all corners. Cut along the trace line. Measure perimeter of the fabric. Cut a piece of ¾"-wide cotton tape to this length. Fold the tape evenly over the raw edge of the fabric, pinning in place as you go. Sew through the tape and fabric, keeping the tape even and watching that the stitching goes through all three layers. Fold the tape under where the ends meet, and slip-stitch. To place the grommet holes, fold a corner on the diagonal. Mark a spot on both sides of the folded fabric that is approximately 3" from the edge and 1" away from the fold. Mark a second spot 2" away from the fold. Insert a grommet at each spot, four to a corner. Thread an 8" length of cotton or silk cord through each set of the grommet holes, as shown. Tie knots in the ends to keep the cord from sliding through. Tie the cord together to cinch the slipcover around the top of the stool, holding the cover in place.

HOW TO MAKE A RUNNER TABLECLOTH

To make the crisscrossed tablecloth on page 48, make two separate runners. For a square table, the runners will be the same size; for a rectangular one, the runners will be different sizes. To determine the lengths of the runners: Start 12" above the floor, measure to the top of the table, continue across the top, and down the other side to within 12" of the floor; repeat in other direction if table is a rectangle. For the widths of the runners: Measure the tabletop from corner to corner, then subtract two inches; repeat in other direction if table is a rectangle. Add 1" to all sides for hem allowance. Cut two pieces of fabric to these dimensions. 1 On each runner, turn under the long sides ¼", then ¾"; press and topstitch. Repeat on the short sides. 2 Center one runner across the other at right angles. Pin, and stitch around the perimeter of the area where the two overlap.

HOW TO MAKE A TERRY-CLOTH COVER

The chartreuse terry-cloth slipcover on page 49 is made from a single bath towel. To make it, first measure the top of your stool. Cut the towel into one large rectangle that covers the seat's top and two sides, plus ½" all around for the seams. Cut two more strips to cover the remaining two sides of the seat, also with ½" for seams. To prevent fraying, finish all raw edges with a zigzag stitch. Make the button tabs as follows: Cut the dobby, the unlooped border near the edge of the towel, into four 4½"-long strips. Fold one strip in half lengthwise, right sides together, and pin. (The towel we used had a very wide dobby; sew two pieces of a narrower dobby together instead of folding.) Sew along the long edge and one short edge of the strip, leaving a ¼" seam allowance. Turn right-side out. Sew a buttonhole the size of your button into the tab. Trim the tab to 3". Repeat to make the remaining three tabs. Lay the large rectangle, right-side up, on a work surface. Center the two strips along the two longer sides of the rectangle, right sides facing and raw edges aligned. Pin together. Starting ½" shy of the end of the strip, sew pieces together, leaving another ½" at the other edge. Pin button tabs to the ends of the strips, where the corners will be. Fold the long edges of the rectangle down to align with the ends of the strips. Pin, and sew, incorporating the tabs in the seam. Turn right-side out. Mark the button placement, and sew on the buttons by hand.

THIS PAGE Handmade wood-veneer shades unite two very different lamps: a cast-iron Arts and Crafts candlestick and a solid-looking alabaster base from the thirties. OPPOSITE An opaque-paper coolie shade funnels light downward onto a beet-red porcelain base and creates a well-illuminated reading area.

Lamps & Shades

Assembling the perfect lamp out of a unique base and a homemade shade

GOOD LIGHTING IS ESSENTIAL TO COMFORTABLE LIVING. BUT LAMPS ARE more than sources of illumination; they are also sculptural objects in their own right, bringing unique forms, colors, and materials to an interior.

A great lamp begins with a striking base, and many can be found at flea markets and antiques shops. Look for appealing shapes and good quality materials; some, like alabaster and mercury glass, are especially lovely when played upon by light. Don't be dismayed if you fall in love with a base that doesn't work—rewiring is usually easier and quicker than finding an equally great one. Buy it, and fix it up instead (see pages 68 and 69 for instructions).

The next step is to choose—or make—the right shade, which will bring the whole piece into balance and harmony. Lamps and their shades should be compatible in three ways: style, shape, and size. Personal taste is your best guide, but a few rules do apply. First, the more formal the base (brass or porcelain, for example), the richer the shade material should be. Silk, fine linen, satin, and velvet are all good choices. As with bases, some shades take on new life when illuminated. Wood veneer, silk, and parchment create a warm, rich glow. Hold materials up to a bulb before buying.

To decide on the shape of a shade, take your cue from the basic geometry of the base. Rounded ones are best suited to rounded shades; square or rectangular bases to paneled shades. Flared paneled shades, which have controlled curves, will work on lamps of just about any shape. A shade must be wide enough to allow the bulb at least an inch of space all around (two inches if the wattage is one hundred or more) and long enough to cover the electrical fittings—but no longer than that, or the shade will look like a hat pulled down too low over the ears.

It's worth the effort to find the perfect shade for every base. Lamps are always noticed: The eye, like the moth, is naturally drawn to their light.

ABOVE This coolie shade, also shown on the previous page, is made from dark-tan paper attached to pressure-sensitive styrene. The top and bottom edges are trimmed with blue-gray bookbinding tape, which adds a sophisticated touch of color to the finished lamp. OPPOSITE Although contemporary, this teak and alabaster base has such a classic form that a traditional Empire shade suits it just fine. Like the coolie shade, this one is made by hand and edged in blue bookbinding tape. The cream-colored paper is slightly more translucent than the khaki, however, so the lamp emits a soft glow in all directions. A beeswax box on the table catches the rays.

HOW TO MAKE A BASIC PAPER SHADE

A shade need not be made from fancy materials to be beautiful. Plain paper makes wonderful shades, as long as the color and proportions are right. The wraparound paper shades on pages 53 and 55 can be made from any paper you like; just be sure to choose one that looks good when illuminated from behind. According to David Aldera, manager of the paper department at New York Central Art Supply, "People bring flashlights to the store when they're looking for lampshade paper. You can't count on the store to have the right kind of light source."

The formula explained here can be adjusted to accommodate any height and slope; experiment by rolling craft paper into cones to get a sense of the proportions that will work best with your lamp base. Determine the height you want your lampshade to be, as well as the diameter of its top and bottom rings; order the rings in those dimensions from a lampshade supplier. Then follow the steps demonstrated in the photos above. 1 All circular shades derive from a pattern in the form of an arc (see the diagram, opposite right); this shape is then penciled onto pressure-sensitive styrene, a flexible translucent polymer that comes with a peel-off paper backing. Using a ruler, draw a line representing the vertical height of the

lampshade (line AB in the diagram) onto the styrene's paper backing. Draw two more lines perpendicular to the top and bottom of this line that represent the diameters of the shade's top (CD) and bottom (EF) rings. Connect points C and E, and continue the line upward the same distance as CE. Repeat with points D and F. Label the intersection of CE and DF as point G. Multiply the length of line EF by pi (3.14); add ½" for an overlap. This measurement represents the length of arc FH, which can be drawn with a yardstick compass. Anchor the compass on point G, and place the pencil on point F. Swing pencil to left, drawing a semicircle. Use a cloth tape measure to check the distance. Repeat process for line CD, multiplying its length by 3.14 and adding ½". This measurement equals arc DI. Draw it with compass anchored on G and pencil placed on D, checking with a cloth tape measure. Cut out the resulting arcs (represented in the diagram by the dotted lines); use scissors for the curves and a utility knife and metal ruler for the straight edges. 2 Choose a decorative paper that is safe to use near a lightbulb. Stick the paper onto the pressure-sensitive styrene, peeling off the backing and laying the decorative paper onto it; begin at one end, and press carefully to avoid air bubbles. Trim

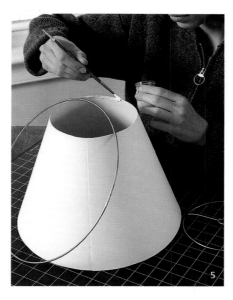

away excess paper from around the pattern with a utility knife. Be careful not to cut into the styrene. 3 With the decorative paper facing out, gently bend the shade into its shape, leaving a ½" overlap. Fit the top ring into the shade, just inside the edge so that the ring and paper are flush at the top; secure with clothespins. Repeat with the bottom ring. Adjust top and bottom of shade until the fit is perfect, with the rings fitting snugly and a ½" overlap remaining on the seam. Using a pencil, trace a line along the inside edge of the seam; remove the clothespins. 4 With a paintbrush, dab a clear-drying craft glue such as Sobo on the styrene in the space between the penciled line and the edge. Bend shade back into shape, and glue along seam. Hold seam in place for a couple of minutes until the glue sets, then clip clothespins at the top and bottom; let shade dry 1 hour. 5 Brush glue along the top inside edge of the shade, about ¼" deep. Insert the top ring, lining up the shade's seam with one of the top ring's three spokes. Clip clothespins all around; repeat with larger ring for bottom of the lampshade. Let glue dry 1 hour; remove clothespins. 6 Choose a stretchy trim such as double-fold bias tape for a more angled style. When using bookbinding tape, cut it to a width of ½". Fold trim along its length. Starting at the seam, adhere it to top and bottom, inch by inch.

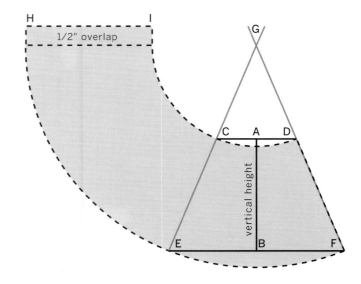

OPPOSITE Whipstitching brings a retro touch to a tall rectangular shade, created to complement the skyscraper form of a forties glass base; a purple Venetian-glass teardrop vase holds springtime branches nearby. Ice-blue silk cord secures the craft-paper shade to a custom-made frame. Because this shade is so tall, it was necessary to replace the lamp's harp with a longer one. When pairing lamp bases and shades, pay attention to the hardware fittings: Most large lamps use harps—metal braces that attach to the base at its neck and to the shade with a screw-in finial on top. To fit onto a harp, a shade must have a washer attachment joined by spokes to the top of its frame. Some shades are constructed with a clip that grips the bulb; these shades need to be refitted before they can be used with a harp. ABOVE LEFT Leather lacing and "elephant-hide" paper give a summer-camp feeling to this whipstitched shade, paired with an American art pottery base. ABOVE RIGHT Holes in an opaque-paper shade form a pattern of light over a contemporary wooden base.

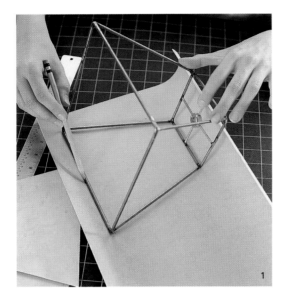

HOW TO MAKE A WOOD-VENEER SHADE

Wood veneer looks especially rich and warm when illuminated. Available from woodworkers' supply shops and catalogs, veneer is surprisingly flexible and easy to work with. Just remember that, like paper, wood does burn. If exposed to high heat over time, it will turn brittle and dry, making it especially flammable. Make sure that your shade will be at least 1" from the bulb on all sides—more if you plan to use a bulb of 100 watts or higher. The shades shown on page 52 were made with bird's-eye maple veneer. To make the square Empire shade: 1 Flatten the veneer. Using a pencil, trace each side of the frame onto the wood. Keep track of corresponding sides of frame and veneer sections by labeling them with masking tape. Cut out the veneer panels with a utility knife, using a metal ruler to keep lines straight. Dab clear-drying craft glue onto the frame with a paintbrush, one side at a time. 2 Press veneer into place; use clothespins to hold until dry, about 1 hour. Cut self-adhesive bookbinding tape in half lengthwise, and cover the edges of the frame: Start with the vertical spines, then top and bottom. To make the drum-shaped lampshade,

purchase two rings equal in diameter. Calculate the circumference by multiplying the diameter by pi (3.14); add ½" for an overlap. Cut veneer into a piece this long, with its width equal to the height you want the shade to be. Bend shade into its shape, leaving ½" of overlap. Fit top ring into shade, so that ring and veneer are flush at the top; secure with clothespins. Repeat with bottom ring. Adjust shade until the fit is perfect, with rings fitting snugly and a ½" overlap on seam. Using a pencil, trace a line along inside edge of seam; remove clothespins. With a paintbrush, dab glue onto overlapping section of seam, between penciled line and edge. Bend shade back into shape, and glue along seam. Hold a few minutes until glue sets, then clip clothespins at the top and bottom; let dry 1 hour. Brush glue inside the top edge of the shade. Insert the top ring, lining up the shade's seam with one of the ring's spokes. Clip clothespins all around; repeat with the bottom ring. After 1 hour hour, remove clothespins. Cut self-adhesive bookbinding tape to a width of ½". Fold it along its length. Starting at the lampshade's seam, adhere it to the top and bottom edges.

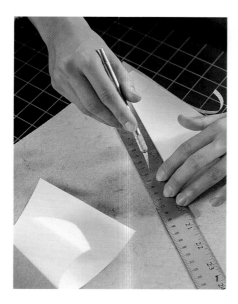

HOW TO MAKE A WHIPSTITCHED SHADE

Whipstitching is one of the easiest ways to securely join a lampshade's panels to its frame. The thick, contrasting seams, made by stitching a cord at an angle through precut holes, enhance a shade's handmade quality. This technique is best suited to papers that have a natural or rustic appearance, such as parchment, or the "elephant-hide" textured paper used here.
1 To make the hexagonal shade on page 59, trace one side of the frame six times onto the paper side of pressure-sensitive styrene. Using a utility knife and a metal ruler, cut out the six shapes. Peel the backing from one section of the styrene at a time, and stick it onto your chosen paper. Use the styrene as a pattern, and trim away the excess paper, being careful not to cut the styrene. 2 Make a template by tracing one piece of the peeled-off backing onto a sheet of cardboard. Draw lines along the cardboard, ¼" in from the edges. Mark points spaced ¼" apart along the lines. Use a ⅛" hole punch to make the holes. Place the template over one section of the shade, mark the holes with a pencil, remove the template, and punch out the holes. Repeat for the other five sections.
3 Stitch the panels onto the frame with suede string, connecting first the top and then bottom edges of all

six. Knot the string behind one corner of a panel; sew around the top, and add the other panels as you go. Knot end on back side of frame. Repeat at bottom. Stitch panels together at the side seams. To make an Empire shade, follow steps 1 through 3 on pages 56 and 57. Unfold, and lay flat; on the back, mark and punch rows of holes, ¼" apart and ¼" in from top and bottom. Along the seam line drawn in step 3, punch a row of holes on each side, ¼" apart and ¼" in from seam. Bend into shape. If holes are blocked, mark with a pencil, open shade, and punch out. Continue steps 5 and 6 on page 57 for a basic paper shade. Once rings have been fitted and glued in place, whipstitch with heavy trim such as silk cord. To make the rectangular frame on page 58, cut a piece of watercolor paper so that one side equals the height of the finished shade. For the length of the paper, multiply the distance of one side of the frame by 4 (measure outside wire); add ½". Score corners with a bone folder. Fold paper in quarters, following frame's shape. Tuck down overlap. Make a cardboard template according to step 2; punch holes at ½" intervals along top and bottom edges. Glue overlap to inside edge. Stitch shade to frame with silk cord.

HOW TO MAKE A PLEATED SHADE

A pleated paper shade is easy to measure and cut out. It begins as a simple rectangle of paper, rather than the precisely measured arc required for some of the shades on the previous pages; a tighter cinch at the top than at the bottom provides its graceful flare. The pleated Empire shade shown opposite starts with a lampshade frame ordered to size. Any heat-resistant, heavy cardstock will do for the shade. Measure the length of the frame from outer edge of top ring to outer edge of bottom ring, then add ¾". This length equals the width of the paper. Multiply the diameter of the bottom ring by pi (3.14); multiply this product by 2.25 to determine the paper's length. Cut the paper to size. Using a ruler and pencil, working on the back side of the paper, lightly draw lines parallel to paper's width at ½" increments. 1 Using a ruler as a guide, score the fold lines by pressing a bone folder into the paper. 2 Cut a small piece of cardboard ½" wide and, using an ⅛" hole punch, make a hole about 1" from the paper's end. Use this template to mark dots along lampshade paper, centering one dot between every pair of scored lines. Punch out dots, then fold and pleat paper at the scored lines, using a ruler to keep the edges straight. Overlap ends, and glue together to close the circle. 3 Set the frame over a block of wood or a jar; thread cord through punched holes all around the shade. Lightly place over the frame, and tighten to fit the top ring (the shade should

extend about ¼" above the frame). Knot the cord on the inside of shade, and trim the excess. 4 Use a small paintbrush to dab glue where the inside pleats touch the frame. Let glue dry for 1 hour, then turn the shade over, and glue the tips of the pleats to the bottom ring. Allow the glue to dry thoroughly.

To make the cylindrical pleated drum lampshade below, measure and cut paper as described above. Instead of scoring the pleats with a bone folder, use a sewing machine without thread to stitch a row of small holes along each pencil line; these holes will emit light when the lamp is illuminated. Using a template, mark and punch holes along the top and bottom edges of each pleat, and thread with raffia.

THIS PAGE A pale and dreamy
bedside lamp is made from a vintage
alabaster base topped with a pink
handmade pleated Empire shade. A silk
cord passes through holes punched in
each pleat, cinching the shade at the
top. A bone folder was used to create
the pleats. The etched water glass and
bottle were found at a flea market
in Paris. OPPOSITE, BOTTOM
LEFT AND RIGHT A pleated shade
suits a more modern interior when it is
shaped into a perfectly cylindrical
drum shape. An unthreaded sewing
machine was used to "stitch" parallel
rows of small dots in the paper, making
the perforations where the pleats fold;
raffia keeps the pleats in place.

THIS PAGE Khaki silk is stretched taut around a flared hexagonal lampshade frame. Satin ribbon in the same color gives it an elegant edge. The sturdiest lampshades aren't glued; they're sewn. And the frame is painted with enamel, so it won't rust and stain the fabric.

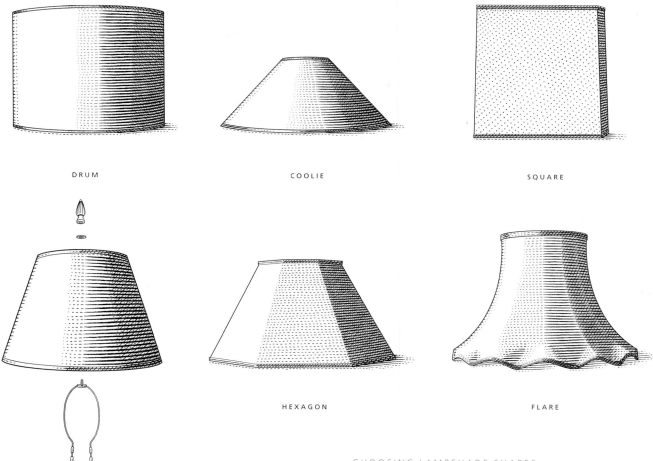

DRUM   COOLIE   SQUARE

HEXAGON   FLARE

EMPIRE

CHOOSING LAMPSHADE SHAPES

Like the cut of a skirt, the shape of a lampshade often evokes a particular era or style. The pure geometry of the drum recalls midcentury modernism; the coolie seems at home in an eighties decorator showhouse; the hexagon has an early-twentieth-century rustic feeling. The material a lampshade is made out of can either play up these references or tone them down—mica and cowhide, for example, were favorites during the Arts and Crafts period; blond wood and aluminum were common in the fifties.

As with fashion, classic shapes transcend fads. The lampshades shown above are basics that will work in a range of interiors. Each style can be made or purchased in a number of variations—taller, wider, more or less sloped. Plain paper and fabric make them the most versatile but need not look dull, since these materials are available in sophisticated colors and textures. Fabric is flexible and can stretch to fit the contours of a frame that is flared or curved, while the best-quality paper has a natural stiffness that allows you to forgo a frame's vertical ribs and use just a top and bottom ring to give it structure.

Ready-made lamps with shades are easy enough to find, but many of the best-looking ones are those you piece together out of components you find or make. Begin with a base— it can be something that was originally designed as part of a lamp, or it can be a vase, urn, or statue. To convert it (left), make sure there is a passageway through the middle so a cord can run from the bottom to the top (see "Rewiring a Lamp," page 68). A tube, attached to the base, keeps the harp holder and socket in place. A harp fits into the harp holder; it reaches up around the bulb to support the shade, which is held in place with a washer and finial.

HOW TO TRIM A SHADE IN VELVET

A simple silk lampshade, purchased at a lighting store, looks chic when trimmed with velvet ribbon. The dark velvet border on the shade shown opposite also makes the ribs, visible through the silk, seem less obtrusive. Other ribbons or trims, such as woven upholstery tape or embroidered lace, work equally well. To trim a lampshade in velvet, cut two lengths of ¼"-wide velvet ribbon slightly longer than the circumferences of the top and bottom of the shade. For the top, apply fabric glue to the back of the ribbon, and align it with the upper edge of the shade so that the edge of the ribbon is flush with the top of the shade; pin ribbon in place with straight pins, to hold in place until the glue dries. Trim the ribbon ends with a vertical cut so that they meet exactly and don't overlap. Repeat for the bottom edge of shade.

HOW TO MAKE A SCONCE SHADE

Some vintage prints are too nice to hide away but not important enough to frame. Turn one into a sconce shade to show it off in a subtle way. The sconce shade shown opposite was made with an old moth print found at a flea market, but the concept works just as well with a vintage map or etching, or with fine wood veneer. 1 To make it, purchase a clip-on wire sconce frame, available from lighting stores. Using a pencil, trace the wire frame onto the back side of the print. Since many frames bow inward at the sides, you may need to true the edges of the drawn shape with a straight-edge in order to create a perfect rectangle. Cut out the print along these lines. On the front of the print, use a pencil and ruler to make a rectangle positioned ¼" in from edges. Lay the print over pressure-sensitive styrene, and trace around print. Cut out styrene. 2 Peel back a 1"-wide strip of the styrene's backing, and align print over it. Peel back the rest of the backing and slowly lay the print in place, smoothing out any wrinkles or air bubbles as you go. 3 Tape shade in place to the wire frame with two pieces of drafting tape at each end. Wrap self-adhesive bookbinding tape over the top and bottom edges of the shade, following the pencil marks to keep the tape straight. Use a razor to trim corners, and remove drafting tape before wrapping ends with bookbinding tape. Mount shade to bulbs on sconce.

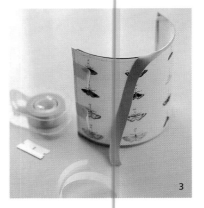

ABOVE LEFT A store-bought silk lampshade is dressed up with velvet ribbon trim, turning it into into an elegant partner for the mercury-glass candlestick lamp base. ABOVE RIGHT A handmade sconce shade shows off a print found at a flea market, framing and illuminating the design, a chart of moths. The frame clips directly onto the bulb, a technique that is best suited to lightweight shades. The frame is covered in pressure-sensitive styrene to which the moth print has been attached. A map or etching would also work well, but be sure to hold the paper up to a light first to see what color it throws when illuminated.

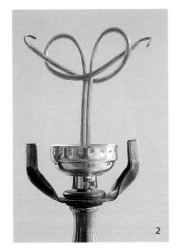

Don't hesitate to buy that wonderful antique lamp at your local auction—if it doesn't work properly, you can just rewire it. And never throw up your hands in despair when a troublesome lamp at home refuses to work. It's not difficult to fix or even completely rewire almost any lamp—and you'll save a lot of money in the process.

The first step is to find the problem. If your lamp doesn't turn on, check that it is plugged into a working outlet and that the bulb is good. Then check the cord and the plug for damage (if the cord is damaged, skip the next paragraph and follow the steps for changing a cord; for more on changing a plug, see "Replacing Plugs," opposite). If the cord looks good, the next step is to test the socket.

Unplug the lamp and remove the lightbulb before testing the socket. Squeeze the socket shell where the word "press" is imprinted, and lift it off the cap (some lamps will have a small setscrew that needs to be loosened before you can lift out the shell). Lift out the insulating sleeve. Loosen the terminal screws, and remove the wires. Use a continuity tester to test the socket: Attach the tester's clip to the metal part of the body, and touch the probe to the silver terminal screw. If the tester lights, the socket is good. The socket switch may be bad, however, so test it next: For a one-way switch, attach the clip to the brass terminal screw; with the switch in the "on" position,

the tester should light when the probe touches to the round tab inside the socket. If the socket or switch is bad, buy a new socket just like the old one. Skip to step 2 in the following paragraph to find out how to rewire the socket.

If the cord is obviously damaged or worn, replace it. If the socket has not been separated from the wires, detach the wires from the terminal screws. Cut the old cord somewhere between the plug and the base of the lamp. Cords comprise two insulated wires, joined at the middle; split the top 2" of the new cord down the middle. Using a wire stripper, remove ½" of insulation from each wire. You may also need to separate and strip the old cord. Twist the old wires and new wires together with a western-union splice, allowing you to guide the new cord into place with the old one. Make an X shape with the two exposed wires; put your finger at the tip of one of the wires, and push it down, wrapping it around the other wire; repeat with the other tip. Continue until you've made a single row of tight little coils (they should look like the coiled rope on a noose). A Western Union splice, when covered with electrical tape, should be able to slip through a lamp or chandelier arm.   Pull carefully at the top of the cord so that the new cord will be threaded through the lamp. When the new cord is visible, disconnect the old cord and discard it.   If there is room in the cap to hold it, tie the ends of the new wire into an underwriter's knot, as shown, which will prevent the cord from being pulled free of the socket by a tug or a jerk at the end of the cord. 3 Wrap the neutral wire (covered with ridged insulation) clockwise around the silver terminal screw; tighten. Wrap the smooth, hot wire clockwise around the brass terminal. and tighten. Test the connections on the socket with a continuity tester. Snap the socket body into place. Replace the insulating cover and the shell. 4 Plug in the newly rewired lamp, and turn it on.

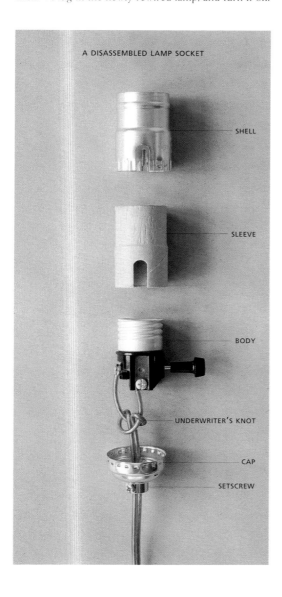

A DISASSEMBLED LAMP SOCKET

SHELL

SLEEVE

BODY

UNDERWRITER'S KNOT

CAP

SETSCREW

REPLACING A PLUG

To attach a new plug to a new or undamaged cord, you can use either a self-clamping plug or a screw-on plug. Self-clamping plugs are simple to install, but they will not accept cords of certain shapes or sizes. You may need to ask for help at an electrical-supply store when matching a plug to a cord. Plugs that are cracked, discolored, or warm to the touch when in use should be replaced. Changing plugs for large appliances can be complicated, so amateurs should change only lamp, radio, clock, or other small appliance plugs.

To install a self-clamping plug (below left), cut off the cord at a right angle (including any damaged parts) near the old plug. Then open the shell of the new plug. Slip the wire in from behind, and clamp the prongs shut; replace the shell. You don't need to strip the insulation from a cord inserted into a self-clamping plug.

To install a screw-on plug (below right), pry the insulating disk from the prongs. Strip the new wire back ½", and solder or twist the strands together tightly. Insert the wire into the plug from behind, and wrap each wire so it goes around a prong for support before it is attached to its terminal screw. Be sure exposed wires do not touch. If the plug is polarized (one prong will be larger than the other), connect the positive wire to the terminal screw of the smaller prong (this should be a brass screw); connect the neutral wire to the silver terminal screw. Replace the insulating disk. Plug in the lamp, and turn it on.

THIS PAGE Newly constructed shelves merge gracefully into the living room of a fifties builder's colonial. Architectural details from both the baseboard and crown molding are carried onto the unit. The shadowy blue-green paint brings a note of intensity to the otherwise pale room and highlights the objects on display. OPPOSITE In the tight area of a front hall, a small shelf offers just enough surface for keys and mail, without encroaching on the limited floor space.

Shelves

Adding color and character along with space for storage and display

ABOVE Inexpensive adjustable shelving disguises its pedigree with a few simple tricks. The wooden shelf platforms have 2³/₄-inch wood trim, painted to match the walls; the metal standards and braces are also painted to match. OPPOSITE The strong horizontal of the same shelves counterbalances the verticality of the books. A few interspersed objects, like the contemporary pottery vase, break up the monotony of the volumes and help create a pleasing visual rhythm on the wall. The lowest shelf hovers three feet above floor level, leaving space for a pair of trunks and a stool by Charles and Ray Eames. The chair and ottoman were designed by Robsjohn-Gibbings in the fifties. On the floor is a contemporary rug from Tibet.

OF COURSE SHELVES CAN ORGANIZE GREAT QUANTITIES OF THINGS. BUT shelves themselves have character all their own, and the best ones bring as much style as they do storage to a room.

There are several things to consider when selecting or designing them. First, they should suit the architecture of the room. They can do this quite literally, by repeating or continuing existing details, like moldings and baseboards. Or they can make more oblique references, echoing the proportions, scale, or sensibility of the space without actually imitating any particular element of it. Shelves should also suit the things they hold. They needn't be the same style or material—a contemporary glass shelf can be used to support a collection of antique bronze figures. But a shelf and its contents should complement one another. A collection of fine porcelain deserves something better than unpainted plywood, for example. And heavy art books should be kept on shelves that are hefty enough to support their weight.

Shelves should use space wisely and economically. Seldom more than fifteen inches deep, they can squeeze into spaces where other furniture won't go. A set of them will turn a slender hallway into a library, or a narrow wall between windows into a place to display a favorite collection. An individual shelf is even more efficient, giving you a surface to hold a lamp or clock exactly where you need it, and keeping the floor free and clear.

Finally, shelves should be tailored to accommodate the idiosyncrasies of your life. Before you build a giant library to house all your books, consider whether two or three medium-size units in the appropriate rooms wouldn't make more sense—one for cookbooks, one for gardening books, one for novels. After all, the real talent of shelves is that they keep things out of the way but close at hand, exactly where you want them to be.

OPPOSITE In a tiny bedroom with very high ceilings and no closets, much-needed storage space is created above the doorway with the addition of a broad shelf that holds a stack of linens and vintage tin boxes. A high entablature marries the shelf with the door frame. Shaker pegs provide a place to hang artwork or hats. The console table has front legs only; the back screws directly into the wall. A nineteenth-century Sheffield silver candlestick is the base for the lamp. ABOVE A wall unit in a narrow dining alcove combines the roles of display and storage. Various shelf heights accommodate an assortment of stained wooden boxes that function like drawers, concealing items too messy or fragile to be left in view. A particularly tall space above the third shelf allows it to serve as a sideboard at mealtime. The chair is by Arne Jacobsen, the table by Charles and Ray Eames. Upholstery fabric from the forties covers the pillow on the sofa.

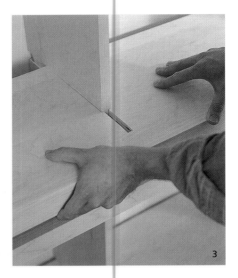

HOW A WALL UNIT IS BUILT

The full-size wall unit shown on page 75, built into a narrow dining alcove that would have been awkward to furnish with a traditional sideboard, looks like the expensive custom work of a carpenter. With a plan both convenient and economical, the shelving has actually been cut to measure for on-site slot-together assembly with a minimum of hardware. 1 The width of the alcove was first measured carefully from bottom to top so that any discrepancies in the dimensions of the room could be accommodated when cutting the lumber. Each piece should be held in place quickly before assembly to ensure that it fits in its proper spot. 2 The vertical boards at each end of the unit are secured to the walls with appropriate anchoring hardware. The bottom shelf rests on several small, aluminum I-beam feet. The two vertical boards in the center fit into mortised grooves in the bottom shelf. 3 Horizontal shelves have precut slots that slide into precut grooves in the vertical boards. With few nails or screws, the gridlike assembly of slotted and grooved boards locks the unit securely in place as it rises on the wall. 4 The narrow sliding boxes provide drawerlike storage for linens and tableware.

Open shelving is only as good as the hardware that holds it up. Determine the type of wall you are dealing with, and select the appropriate hardware; consult your local supplier or a carpenter if you're uncertain. As a general rule, drywall or wallboard necessitates toggle bolts, which enter the drill holes, then open and anchor behind the wall, securing the hardware. Plaster walls also require toggle bolts; alternately, find the studs behind the plaster, and sink standard screws into those. Brick or stone walls require that screws be set into lead or plastic anchors. Though metal standards and braces—the ubiquitous shelving hardware—might seem plain, the shelves themselves can provide a little style, with an unusual choice of either material or trim. Easily found options include (right, top to bottom):

- ½" frosted glass
- ¾" wood with astragal, an ornate half-round trim
- 1¼" rough-hewn clear red oak with a wax finish
- ¾" wood with a nose-and-cove trim
- ¾" wood with a ½" round at the edge
- ¾" composition board covered in linen with a binding-tape edge
- ¾" veneer plywood with a matching iron-on veneer-tape edge
- ½" clear glass with a 1½" glass facing edge
- stainless-steel professional-kitchen shelf, available from restaurant-supply stores

LEFT In a frequently used family room, a wall of shelves makes the most of the spaces between, beside, and beneath two large windows. Built off-site as three separate units, the shelves were installed and finished on-site, with high-impact details like nose-and-cove trim attached to the counter and crown molding extended across the top. The window-seat cushions are upholstered with vintage mattress ticking. Baskets under the seats hold toys for the family's two sons. The Scottish bobbin chairs are from the nineteenth century. The coffee table is made from the enamel base of a stove from the twenties, painted white and fitted with a linen-covered top.
ABOVE A rounded bump-out on the top shelf holds a Keith Murray Wedgwood vase from the thirties.

The full wall of shelving shown on pages 78 and 79 is made up of three basic framed box units built off-site and finished with simple molding and trim. Having the bulk of the work produced at a wood shop instead of having a carpenter do custom work on-site cuts costs considerably. 1 Each of the units fits either between wall and window or window and window. The basic cabinets have setbacks— the top shelves are shallower—providing waist-high surfaces with deeper shelves below for storing oversize books. 2 The gap between the wall and cabinet results from the baseboard molding already in the room; once the units are in place, a piece of lath trim finishes the cabinets flush to the wall. 3 Nose-and-cove molding on the edge of the counter adds another detail that makes the shelves appear like furniture. 4 Each of the two window seats is actually a 1¼"-thick wooden shelf that rests on wooden supports between the cabinets; another shelf runs close to the floor beneath the seat. 5 Pegs fit into holes drilled into the sides of the cabinet to make the shelves adjustable, a useful modification for a built-in unit whose uses can be expected to change over the years. 6 The cabinets are finished at the base with a board that runs the unit's length; arched cutouts make cleaning easier and provide furniture-like feet that lighten the visual load of the unit.

THIS PAGE Not all shelves have to be versatile. This unit was designed for a single purpose: to house a collection of Wedgwood drabware. Hung in a dining room, it is both decorative and functional. Dowels and grooves at the back of each shelf hold plates and platters in place. Shelves are painted to match the wall color, with trim that matches the china. OPPOSITE In Martha's Westport garden room, new shelves look right at home because they match the architectural details of existing door moldings. Velvet-covered boards line the bottoms and backs of the upper three shelves to protect and highlight fragile French porcelain.

OPPOSITE Widely spaced shelves held up by graphic, wrought-iron braces silhouette a clean-lined collection. The shelves are covered with linen, which protects the pottery against chipping and is an attractive alternative finish if you'd rather wield a staple gun than a paintbrush. A spherical Keith Murray Wedgwood vase holds the place of honor at the center of the group. Two alabaster bowls sit above, and a pair of alabaster pots occupies the lowest shelf; all other pieces are art pottery from the thirties and forties. The stark English Arts and Crafts chair is from the 1880s. ABOVE LEFT The underside of shelves is often as important as the front or top. With these vintage ceramic brackets, the shelves become objects of display in their own right. Originally designed to hold individual porcelain treasures, these brackets now support pieces of coral. ABOVE RIGHT Antique cast-iron braces support a slab of travertine marble beside a bed, supplying a surface for a clock and lamp without cluttering the serene expanse of floor space. The slender bed, made from a Shaker kit, also appears to float. When heavy materials such as marble are used as shelves, the braces should be anchored securely to the wall with toggle bolts or expansion bolts, depending on the wall material. Check with a stone yard or fabricator for details, and ask how wide a distance such stone can span between supports.

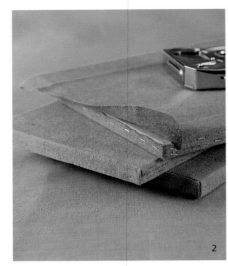

HOW TO COVER SHELVES WITH FABRIC

The appearance of a shelf can be softened without losing its crisp line on the wall by covering the platform with fabric, such as heavy painter's linen. The set of widely spaced linen-dressed shelves shown on page 85 keeps a pottery collection on view, out of harm's way, and readily accessible. Dramatically scaled contemporary wrought-iron brackets complete the decorative effect. Inexpensive plywood provides the base for a shelf platform that will not warp. Cut the linen to measure twice the width of the board plus 2". The length should equal the board's length plus 3". 1 Staple one long edge of the linen along the length of the board, then wrap the fabric around the board, bringing it up to the stapled edge. Stretch tightly for a smooth surface, then staple along the length again. Trim the excess fabric; this will be the back edge of the shelf, facing the wall. 2 At the ends, stretch and staple one fabric edge to the board, then pull other fabric edge over it; pin along edge with pushpins. Neatly fold and tuck remaining fabric, as shown. 3 Glue the tucked edge in place, and secure with another row of pins. Leave the pins in place until the glue has dried. Mount the brackets to the wall, and then place shelves on top.

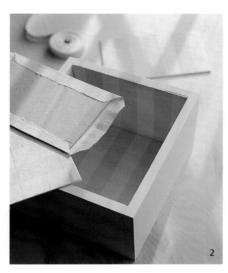

HOW TO MAKE A SHADOW BOX

The sidepieces of the boxes shown on page 88 are made from four pieces of ½" pine. Two of the sidepieces measure 6½" by 4½"; the other two measure 8" by 4½". The back piece, made from ¼" pine, is 8" by 7". 1 Lay the back piece on a flat surface. Spread wood glue along perimeter of back piece, and place the four sidepieces on top. Let glue dry, and secure corners with finishing nails. Turn upside down, and secure back piece to sides with finishing nails. Paint the outer surfaces of the box. 2 To line the box with fabric (we used silk, but any lightweight material will do), measure the inside of back panel; cut a piece of cardstock to that size, subtracting ⅛" from each side to allow for the thickness of silk. Drop this panel into box to be certain it fits with a slight margin all around it. Cut a piece of silk to match dimensions of cardstock, adding 2" to each side. Iron the silk. Center

cardstock on silk. Trim excess fabric by cutting away triangles of silk from corners. Lay a strip of double-sided tape along back edge of card-stock. Pull the silk over edge of that side, and press it onto tape to secure; repeat on the remaining two sides, using a bone folder or knife tip to tuck in excess fabric at corners. Glue the silk-lined panel into bottom of the box. Measure and cut cardstock into panels for the inside walls (leaving a ⅛" allowance for silk on all sides); attach silk to cardstock as described above. Glue silk-lined sidepieces to inside of box. 3 With a paintbrush, apply clear-drying craft glue to the front edges of the sidepieces. Folding corners on the bias as you go, lay ½" woven linen tape (choose a color that complements the silk) along the glued edges. Smooth with a bone folder. Attach two D-rings to the back of the box, and mount two picture hooks on wall, and hang the box.

OPPOSITE In a hushed and monochromatic dining room, the inside wall of a display niche contributes a shock of delicious color. Painted salmon pink, it calls attention to the collection of drabware and jasperware it houses. Built when the house was constructed in the forties, the shelves have shaped contours and grooved surfaces, indicating that they were made to show off an assemblage of fine china; the restrained arrangement here probably looks more modern than what would have originally filled the alcove. The curtains, of khaki-colored twill, are backed with coral-pink lining fabric. A japanned Queen Anne–style chair from the twenties sits against the wall, beneath a mirrored sconce. The Louis XVI–style chair is upholstered in rust-colored velvet. The hen's-foot pattern wool rug was woven in Tibet. In the window, dendrobium and lady's slipper orchids soak up the sun. ABOVE LEFT A collection need not be rare or costly to warrant special attention. A shallow wooden shadow box transforms items found on walks in the woods and on the beach into an ever-changing composition. Handblown pony glasses placed on some of the shelves give shape to groupings of leaves and nuts. Porcupine quills are gathered in a blown-glass tumbler nearby. ABOVE RIGHT A budding collector's first acquisitions of nineteenth-century transferware gain prominence when each object sits in its own box shelf. The handmade wooden boxes are lined with cardstock wrapped in striped silk and finished with linen tape.

THIS PAGE In a spacious entry hall, a transparent folding screen creates a sense of enclosure without blocking light from the rooms beyond. The screen is made of four leaded-glass windows salvaged from the house in which the apartment's owner grew up. The twenties sofa is covered in Fortuny silk; a French side chair is tucked into one angle of the screen. OPPOSITE Beveled mirrors hinged in booklike pairs multiply the effect of candlelight and roses.

Screens & Mirrors

Reshaping interiors with furnishings made to reveal or conceal

ABOVE Plain wooden panels painted five different colors and joined together create a waist-high barrier that discourages little creatures from getting into trouble.
OPPOSITE Afternoon sun streams into Martha's East Hampton library, where a pair of three-panel linen screens acts as occasional cabinet doors to shield her collection of art, architecture, and gardening books from the damaging light. Constructed from artists' canvas stretchers, the lightweight screens can be folded and put away to make way for evening entertaining. On top of the shelves, two McCoy pots hold dendrobium orchids.

SOME FURNISHINGS FILL SPACE; OTHERS RESHAPE IT. WITH SCREENS AND mirrors, you can change the contours of a room, multiply or divide the effects of light and floor space, and offer totally new perspectives.

Like windows, mirrors let you gaze beyond the surface of a wall. They can relieve the claustrophobia of a narrow hallway or a tiny room. But, like windows, not every view a mirror frames is desirable. When placing mirrors, be sure to consider what they reflect. One that picks up a doorway or staircase will offer more architectural interest than one that reiterates a blank expanse. A mirror that reflects a light-filled window brightens a long, dark room. All mirrors need not offer dramatic architectural effects; small ones can act like framed pictures, adding decorative interest. A small mirror can also be positioned to reflect a bouquet or lighted candle. And, of course, mirrors in bathrooms and foyers allow you to inspect yourself before the world casts its eyes on you.

In some ways screens are the opposite of mirrors, since they close off space and interrupt views. But screens are surprisingly versatile. A porch screen made from louvered shutters welcomes breezes while providing privacy; a glass-paned foyer screen does just the reverse, stopping drafts while leaving open the view into the rooms beyond. Screens can create instant retreats, turning a bedroom corner into a dressing room, or an exposed desk into an enclosed study. And they can act as temporary window shades or doors in rooms that have neither.

Screens can also be used as pure deception—to hide those untidy corners or cover unsightly pipes. Yet always be aware that wherever screens are used as masks, they invite curiosity about what lies behind them. After all, that's the real magic of both screens and mirrors: Your imagination will always wander beyond their surfaces.

LEFT Martha doesn't use curtains in her East Hampton bedroom, only a tall, translucent folding screen that blocks views from the front of the house while allowing in the morning sun. The screen also divides the large space into separate areas for working and relaxing. Made from an exterior-shutter kit, the screen has been fitted with linen curtains and green milk-glass panels. The Victorian oak bed and Duncan Phyfe–style chair were both painted white to keep the mood light. The rug is made of linen. ABOVE The same screen used to block a doorway on page 92 here stands sentinel at the end of a hall, shielding a hot radiator without blocking the flow of light or heat into the room.

CHOOSING HINGES

Hinges come in a wide variety of sizes, styles, and materials. Hardware stores carry the basic hinges, but look to furniture-maker suppliers and reproduction-hardware catalogs for more unusual designs. Double-action hinges (above left), which fold in both directions, make the most flexible screens. But they only work if the plate is exactly the same width as the thickness of the panel, since the hinge has to pivot along both edges. For very large, heavy screens, consider loose-pin hinges, which can be taken apart by pulling out the pin, enabling you to easily move or store the screen. Before installing any hinge, decide whether you want the plate to sit flush with the screen's surface or to sit on top. A recessed hinge (above right) has a more finished look and creates a narrower gap between panels, but it is trickier to mount. First, determine the position of the hinge. Do this carefully; the hinge knuckle must be perfectly parallel to the edge of the screen, or the panels will not fold easily back and forth. Trace the outline of the plate, then cut out the perimeter using a mallet and chisel; the chisel's bevel should face toward the bed, the area you'll carve out. Turn the chisel over, so the bevel faces downward; shave out the bed, going in the direction of the wood grain, to the exact thickness of the plate; check after each pass to see if the hinge fits. Place the hinge in the bed, and mark the position of the screws. Drill pilot holes, and install the screws.

HOW TO MAKE A LINEN SCREEN

To make the pair of linen screens shown on page 93, you'll need to make six individual panels. Each one is made from a heavy-weight wooden stretcher, the same kind used for painting canvases, and then covered on both sides with artist's linen. These panels measure 1" by 18" by 40". The stretchers and linen are both available from art-supply stores. 1 Assemble the stretchers, installing center braces across the middle. Cut twelve pieces of linen to fit the frames, adding 2" all around to make stretching easier. 2 Cover both sides of each panel with linen. Start with two staples in the middle of one long side. Pull the opposite side taut; staple twice again. Repeat process with the shorter sides. On each side, staple outward to the corners—smoothing, pulling, and stapling for even tension across the face of the panel. Cover reverse side. 3 Trim any excess linen on all four sides. Cover the stapled edges with twill binding tape, affixing with fabric glue. Repeat steps 2 and 3 with other two panels. 4 Connect three panels with stainless-steel double-action hinges.

HOW TO MAKE A GLASS SCREEN

The ceiling-height bedroom screen on page 94 consists of four individual panels with linen curtains and opaque-glass inserts. The panels' frames actually came from exterior window-shutter kits (see the Guide). The individual pieces are precut, mortised, and tenoned with wood pegging, so they can be easily assembled without heavy tools. We specified four 24"-by-66" (1¼" thick) frames only, without the standard solid-wood inserts for the tops and bottoms. 1 In the bottom of each frame, install a 22"-square piece of ⅛"-thick opaque-green milk glass. The glass sits directly in a groove in the frame; fit precut molding strips around both the front and back of the glass, holding it in place. Further secure the molding with dabs of wood glue at each corner where they fit into the frame; take care not to glue any wood surface to the glass panel. Prime, sand, and paint the wood; we used two coats of a soft white in an eggshell finish. We requested that the top openings come ungrooved from the manufacturer, since this is where the curtains are. Measure the opening, and cut linen to fit, adding 1" on all sides. On both the right and left sides of the curtain, double-turn ½" to the reverse, press, and stitch. On the top and bottom, make a channel 1" wide to accommodate a brass rod to hold the curtain within the frame. Make three more curtains. 2 Hold one of the curtains up to a frame, and mark where the rod should be; mount barrel brackets according to manufacturer's instructions. Attach remaining curtains. Connect two panels with three large brass double-action hinges, placed 11" in from both top and bottom, and 22" apart. Join other pair of screens with three other hinges, then connect all four panels with three more hinges.

HOW TO MAKE A LOW WOOD SCREEN

The easiest way to make a folding screen is to let the lumberyard do most of the work. The screen on pages 92 and 95 is constructed of five 1"-by-12" clear-pine boards (below). Have the boards cut to any length you like; these are 42". Remember that solid wood is heavy, so the longer the panels, the more awkward the screen will be to move. Sand and prime the boards. Let dry, and lightly sand again before applying two coats of paint. You can paint each panel a different color, as we did here with paints from Martha's Araucana collection, including Araucana Turquoise, Oceana, Araucana Sage, and Araucana Blue. Or you can give your screen a unified appearance with a single color. (Semigloss or eggshell finishes will be the most durable and will give the finished creation a soft polish.) Connect two panels with two ¾" double-action hinges (brass or brass plated). Mount them 12" in from both top and bottom. Connect all the screens with hinges. Use two rubber-ball "feet" tacked into the bottom of each panel to protect floors from any scratches. Place the feet 1" in from the corners.

OPPOSITE A bathroom screen punctuated with tiny portholes protects a bather's modesty. Set on casters, it can roll into place to act as a window curtain or to form a temporary dressing room. Grommets pierce the boards, forming a gridlike pattern of light. Installed on a claw-foot tub, which is a refinished antique, is a new chrome hand-held shower, useful for rinsing off after a bath. ABOVE LEFT On a front porch overlooking a busy street, a pair of screens made from louvered exterior-window shutters offers shade and seclusion without stifling summer breezes. During an evening meal at an outdoor table, the screens gracefully shelter candlelight from breezes. The shutters were found at an architectural salvage yard; the wooden legs were attached to add height and architectural interest to the screens. An Adirondack chair, perfect for reading, is made more comfortable with a striped-canvas pillow. ABOVE RIGHT A bedroom desk is hidden from a hallway view by a refurbished nursery screen. The flea-market purchase was repainted, then covered with maps on one side; the reverse, covered with cork, serves as a bulletin board. A nineteenth-century French parlor chair upholstered in a large-scale gingham faces the door.

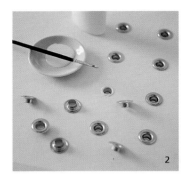

HOW TO MAKE A SHUTTER SCREEN

To make the porch screen on page 99, louvered exterior-window shutters were hinged together in pairs. These shutters, originally from a Gothic Revival house, were found at an architectural-salvage shop; this project will work with any style of shutter, old or new. We cleaned these with a mild detergent, instead of repainting them, because the slightly worn finish adds to their rustic charm. Since the edges where the pairs of panels meet are not flat, the large single-action hinges used to join them had to be attached to the back of the panels. Elevating the screens above the floor makes them appear more graceful, and also provides privacy at eye level, where it's wanted most. The wooden stands (below) are constructed of two-by-two lumber. To make them, cut one piece of wood to the width of the panel, and cut two more to the height you want the legs to be. Then attach mitered cross braces for support. To complement the character of the shutters, we painted the stands with watered-down latex paint, for a whitewashed effect.

HOW TO MAKE A BATHROOM SCREEN

The rolling screen on page 98 is made from three wide panels that have been painted and waxed; each one has a decorative grid of grommets, generally used with heavy canvas. You'll need twice as many grommets as there are holes since only the male halves can be used. Have ¾"-thick veneered plywood cut to measure; these are 14" by 41". Finish the raw edges by ironing on matching veneer tape. Design the grommet pattern, and drill holes the same diameter as the grommet flanges at the ends of the panels. 1 Prime, sand, and paint the panels; we used white matte paint for the bottom two-thirds and a cream semigloss for the tops. Buff the dried paint with Butcher's Wax (see "Enamel and Waxed-Latex Finishes," page 46). 2 Carefully apply a ring of wood glue to a hole and grommet flange; insert a male grommet into each side of the hole. Repeat with remaining grommets. 3 These 1¼" wheel casters come with plastic sleeves. Drill a hole into the bottom corner of each panel, and insert the sleeve. The caster's leg will fit securely into it. 4 Join the panels with double-action hinges.

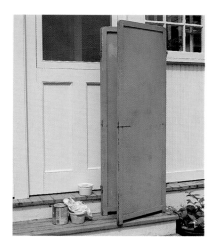

HOW TO REFINISH A NURSERY SCREEN

When found at a flea market, this nursery screen was painted pale blue and decorated with many playroom decals; structurally it was still in good shape, making it a good candidate for a new role as a home-office screen. 1 Before refurbishing an old screen, separate the panels. If the hinges still work, simply strip the paint, and lubricate them with WD40 or a similar lubricant. If the hinges don't work, obtain new ones. Scrape off any peeling paint from the frames, and sand smooth. Prime, lightly sand, and apply two coats of paint. 2 Reface the panels' insets; for this screen, we covered one side with maps, the other with cork. The maps are U.S. Geological Survey topographical maps of Long Island; other maps at the same scale are available for every region of the United States. It took several maps to cover this screen, lining them up edge to edge so that they form one continuous image of the area. Lay the maps out on a large flat surface, cut them precisely to size with a utility knife, and attach to the insets with paper glue thinned with water. Smooth the maps flat, and press into the corners; trim away any excess paper with a utility knife. Apply cork to the other side, so it can be used as a bulletin board near the desk; the cork comes in rolls from office-supply stores. Cut and glue the cork in place just like the maps, but use wood glue instead of paper glue. Put the hinges back on, and put the refurbished screen to good use (right).

OPPOSITE A massive mirror suggests an open doorway in a narrow hall, lending a compelling perspective to the scene. The frame was inspired by four wooden corner blocks from old door frames—found at an architectural-salvage shop. Refinished, they serve as corner pieces. The sides were custom ordered from a wood shop to match. The ¼-inch-thick mirror glass is an investment in itself, costing approximately $800. But nothing else brings as much drama to a quiet space, and the project still costs considerably less than a middling antique pier mirror. The walls are covered with grass cloth, a vintage rag rug lines the floor, and an Art Deco stool beside the stairway collects mail and newspapers. ABOVE Bookbinding cloth folded over the edges of a tall rectangular mirror creates a subtly elegant showpiece. The frame's proportions echo the width of the vertical lattice strips in the wood paneling behind. Three Comice pears ripen in a twentieth-century bronze bowl set atop a turn-of-the-century American console. The vase is an early blown-glass gin bottle.

HOW TO MAKE A HALLWAY MIRROR

The hallway mirror on page 102 has the proportions of a large door: 52" by 79". The frame was actually inspired by wooden corner blocks (below) that were once the corner pieces of a door casing. Look for blocks such as these at architectural-salvage shops; peeling paint doesn't matter as long as the wood has not cracked or split. First, restore the blocks; scrape off old paint, and sand them smooth. Prime, lightly sand, and repaint them. We took the four blocks to a cabinetmaker to have the four sidepieces of the frame constructed to match the profiles of the blocks. Because the dimensions of the top and bottom blocks may not be the same, as is the case here (the top ones are 8½" by 8¾", and the bottom ones are 8½" by 10½"), the widths of the sidepieces will vary. These sidepieces have raised beveled planks in the middle, which vary in width to maintain the overall proportions; two small strips of molding are glued in place on either side. Have mirror glass cut to fit the opening, adding ½" all around; make sure the glass is ¼" thick (any thinner, it will warp and wobble). Prime and paint the frame. To secure the glass in place, screw a cleat, or little ledge, onto the back of the frame, along the bottom edge. Rest the glass upon this ledge; secure glass on other three sides with mirror clips, inserted every 12".

HOW TO MAKE A CLOTH-FRAMED MIRROR

A mirror doesn't have to be encased in a traditional wooden structure. With buckram bookbinding cloth, you can attach a simple fabric "frame" directly to the glass. The cloth is available in a variety of colors and textures from librarians' and bookbinders' supply stores. Have a glazier cut ¼"-thick mirror glass to the size you want. Give the finished piece heft and substance by attaching layers of ¼"-thick foam board, available from art-supply stores, to the back. Using a utility knife, cut three pieces of foam board the same dimensions as the glass, and glue the three together with paper glue. Cut the book-binding cloth into strips that are 4" longer than the dimensions of the glass and 4" wide—allowing a 2" band to frame the mirror, 1" to wrap around the side, and 1" to fold over onto the back. Place the two longer strips on either side of the mirror, and crease the edges sharply. Brush the back side of the fabric with Sobo glue, an all-purpose fabric glue. Allow to dry for 5 to 10 minutes, until sticky; press cloth to the glass, around the edge, and onto the foam board. Trim the fabric to meet the corners exactly. Glue on the top and bottom pieces; trim the fabric, leaving 1"extra at ends. Fold the corners neatly into place, glue flat, and trim any excess.

HOW TO MAKE A FOLDING MIRROR

The tabletop mirror on page 91 appears to unfold in one continuous zigzag, but it is actually three pairs of framed mirrors, joined like books and then arranged end to end. (In order to make this mirror in one long piece, it would have been necessary to attach hinges to both the fronts and backs of the frames, detracting from the final appearance.) The six frames are inexpensive stock pine frames. Lightly sand them, and stain them black with a water-based wood stain. Join each of the three pairs together with 1" butt hinges, secured to the backs. When buying hinges, make sure to choose ones that match the thickness of the frame. Insert the mirror glass; we used ³⁄₁₆"-thick glass that has been beveled by a glazier (see "About Beveling," right). To secure the mirrors inside each frame, cut thin lattice strips (above left) to fit the sides of the rabbet, and screw them inside the back. For the feet, attach silvered glass beads to bottoms of frames with small tacks; make sure the tacks' heads are big enough to hold beads in place.

ABOUT BEVELING Beveling is the process of grinding and polishing the edges of a piece of glass, creating an angle that refracts light. The result gives an elegant, important look to any mirror. According to Marie Zecca, of Zecca Mirror & Glass in New York City, to create a 2"-wide bevel, the glass must be at least ³⁄₁₆" thick to begin with. Most bevels are pretty shallow—the standard angle is about 15°. A more abrupt 45° bevel, called a miter bevel, creates a dramatic prismlike play of light. Because this kind of bevel is ground from the front surface of the mirror to the back, it creates a razor-sharp edge. Before having a mirror beveled, consider the frame: If the frame overlaps the front of the mirror by ½", a 2" bevel will appear only 1½" wide; a ¾" bevel will all but disappear. Having mirrors beveled isn't inexpensive; it can easily double the cost of the mirror glass, and the price goes up if the mirror is round or oval. Old mirrors can be beveled, but be aware that the process may flake off some of the original silver on the back of the mirror, leaving spots.

THIS PAGE An oval looking glass pierced with two holes hangs like a pendant on a bedroom wall, suspended by satin ribbon from the picture rail. The wide bevel is as effective as a wood frame. OPPOSITE, CLOCKWISE FROM TOP LEFT An overmantel mirror, which traditionally included a mirror and picture within one frame, pairs mirrored glass with architectural moldings in a more modern version. An old metal letter from a Woolworth's sign frames a bathroom mirror. A deep and wide frame surrounds a small antiqued mirror that artfully reflects two seedpods from a Chinese lantern plant. Even the smallest foyer will handle doorway traffic more efficiently with the help of a mirrored shelf; the narrow ledge holds mail, keys, and change.

HOW TO MAKE AN OVERMANTEL MIRROR

The overmantel mirror shown on page 103 was made from a wooden-shutter kit and preformed composition-wood-fiber parts, including medallions and beading. Composition wood is commonly used for architecture and furniture detailing; once the flexible pieces have been sanded and painted, they look like intricately carved wood. Before custom ordering the frame (see the Guide), we measured the medallions precisely; the panel at the top of the frame was designed to hold six, arranged side by side. The ¼"-thick mirror glass is a perfect square; a side equals the length of the six medallions positioned together. Before assembling the mirror, sand and prime all the wooden parts. Insert the glass into the frame. Tighten and straighten the frame around the glass, using a carpenter's square to create right angles at all corners. Secure the glass in place with the precut molding strips, which are part of the kit and fit onto both sides of the mirror. Attach the strips with small dabs of wood glue at the corners; take care not to get any glue on the mirror itself. Affix the composition ornaments to the frame (above) with wood glue. The medallions may buckle slightly; press gently in place with a smooth-bottomed glass until the glue dries. Cut beaded trim to fit with a utility knife. Allow glue to dry 24 hours; prime, lightly sand, and paint the frame, using painter's tape on the glass.

HOW TO MAKE A DEEP-FRAMED MIRROR

Each side of the wide, deep frame of the mirror on page 107 is as wide as the mirror glass. To construct the frame, you'll need four pieces of clear-pine or poplar board (1¼"-by-12" stock) that have been miter-cut at a 45° angle on each end. 1 Assemble the parts into a frame, securing each corner with a pair of 1½" corner brackets; mount the inner bracket two inches back from the opening. To give shadow-box depth to the frame, install a second, smaller frame behind it. Make this with standard 1"-by-2" wood strips, miter-cut at 45°. Attach the second frame flush with the opening using countersunk 1½" wood screws. 2 The front has an additional finishing detail: a raised panel formed by four pieces of ¼"-thick clear-pine or poplar lattice, also with mitered corners, attached with wood glue. Seal any cracks and spaces between the mitered joints with plastic-wood filler, then apply several layers of gesso, available at art-supply stores, sanding between each layer. Prime the frame, lightly sand, and apply two coats of paint. Have a glazier cut a piece of ¼"-thick antiqued mirror ½" larger than the opening all around; attach to back of smaller frame with mirror clips.

HOW TO MAKE A MIRROR SHELF

To make the shelf shown on page 107, purchase an unfinished 16"-by-20" wood frame (available at art-supply and framing stores) with a 1¾"-wide molding. Using a drill with a spade bit, counterbore three evenly spaced holes ½" from the bottom on the back of the frame; each hole should be about ¼" deep. Next, construct the shelf. Cut a 1⅛"-thick board to 3½" by 17½"; trim the front and sides with 1⅛" astragal molding. 1 Use a miter box to make perfectly angled cuts for mitered corners; use it to cut the molding ends that meet at front corners of shelf. Cut the front piece first: Starting with a molding piece several inches longer than you need, lay it in the miter box as it would be attached to the shelf, and cut one end. From that cut end, measure the length of the shelf; mark that point on the molding using a combination square, which allows you to mark a 45° angle. Line up the mark with a groove in the miter box, and cut along it. It's easy to end up with a piece that is just too long or just too short; it's better to err on the side of being too long—the molding can be sanded down later. For each sidepiece, use the miter box to make a cut at one end of a piece of molding, hold it up to its place on the shelf, and mark the other end; make a 90° cut. Attach the front piece of the molding to the shelf using four-penny finishing nails every few inches, then the sidepieces; don't set the nails in all the way until you're sure each piece is properly aligned. If mitered ends don't meet perfectly, sand them down, or add wood filler as necessary. 2 Attach the shelf to the frame with 1⅝" drywall screws, inserted into predrilled holes, using a drill with a Phillips-head bit. Start in the center, and insert all screws. 3 The trim around the frame and lip of shelf is ¼"-by-½" lattice. The corners at the top and the front are mitered, but they don't have to be. Measure and miter, if desired, as described above for the molding. Attach the pieces using ½" wire brads every few inches; don't nail within 2" of the ends (the wood could split). Use wood filler to seal any gaps; sand any rough spots. Prime the wood, sand it lightly, then paint it any color you like. 4 Have a glazier cut mirror glass to fit exactly inside the frame. Lay it into the frame, and secure it with two glazier's points on each side: Place a scrap of paper onto the back of the mirror to keep the point from scratching it, and push the point into place with a flat-head screwdriver. Hang the mirror using the appropriate picture-hanging hardware (see page 16).

THIS PAGE Touches of pink have a big impact in an otherwise neutral interior. A cashmere blanket and a few plump pillows covered in vintage ticking bring a blush of life to a scheme of browns, beiges, and whites. The room's rough, natural textures—rattan, sisal, and wicker—are also softened by these plush accessories. OPPOSITE A silk pillow edged in moss fringe perches on a turn-of-the-century French armchair, echoing the pink silk lining of the curtains.

Pillows & Throws

Introducing comfort, color, and pattern with easy fabric projects

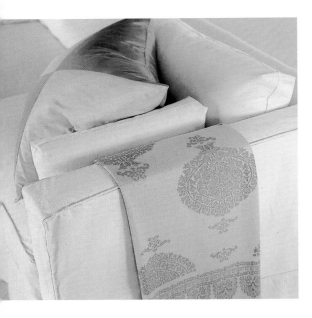

ABOVE An Italian wool-and-silk throw drapes over the arm of an inexpensive sofa upholstered in white cotton, lending an air of sophistication. OPPOSITE A Tuxedo–style sofa, its arms the same height as its back, has clean architectural lines that are emphasized by trim box cushions. They were handmade to replace the jumble of throw pillows that came with the sofa. Ordinary bed pillows stuff the back and arm cushions' cases, shaped by box seams at the corners. Feather-and-down filling makes the sofa feel as luxurious as furniture costing three times as much. Oversize silk harlequin pillows lounge in the corners. An antique glass bee catcher sits on the Paul McCobb coffee table; the fifties lamp is by T.H. Robsjohn-Gibbings.

IT'S THE SOFT THINGS IN A ROOM THAT MAKE YOU WANT TO SETTLE IN and spend time there. Cushions, pillows, and blankets coddle and comfort. Their role isn't purely sybaritic—they are also powerful decorating tools that can quickly transform an interior, shifting a color palette, altering proportions, or adding a stroke of sophistication just where it's needed.

Fabric offers instant luxury. You "feel" it with your eyes as soon as you walk into a room: the soft touch of velvet, the warmth of wool, the cool, dry weight of silk. An inexpensive sofa suddenly looks sumptuous with a cashmere throw draped over it. And pillows covered in ticking or vintage embroidery lend charm to a classic armchair.

Pillows and throws are also an easy way to bring unexpected color into an interior. Perhaps you have a secret fondness for pink or tangerine. You can indulge your decorating sweet tooth without sacrificing a whole room to it. Cover a few pillows in the color; their vivacity can alter the entire room, invigorating neutrals or balancing other strong colors. A change of seasons often brings a craving for different colors and textures, too. Winter's rich wools and velvets give way to bright, breezy linens and cottons in spring. It's easy to store seasonal wardrobes for your furniture in a closet or cupboard.

Replacing the cushions that come with a sofa or chair can offer even more dramatic benefits, correcting unwanted lines and proportions. An overstuffed cream puff of a sofa, for example, might want the tailoring of slim, geometric cushions instead of the shapeless originals. To get a feel for the potential of your upholstered furnishings, remove the cushions and arrange pillows and rolled-up blankets in their place.

The real beauty of pillows and throws lies in the freedom they give you. You can invest in simple, basic furniture in versatile neutrals, then dress it up a dozen different ways with potent touches of texture and color.

HOW TO MAKE A KNIFE-EDGE PILLOW

Many of the pillows in this chapter are variations on the basic knife-edge pillow and can be covered in a variety of fabrics. Each one can be made simply with a cover that is sewn shut by hand. Or they can be made with an opening in the back that can be buttoned or zipped closed, so that the pillowcase can be removed for laundering. For the first type of pillow, begin with two pieces of fabric cut to identical dimensions—the size of the final pillow cover plus 1" for the seam allowance. To make a 16"-square pillow cover, for example, cut two 17" squares of fabric. Pin together, right sides facing with raw edges aligned. Sew the fabric together along three sides, ½" from the edges. Turn right-side out, and press. Insert a 17" pillow (using a pillow insert that's slightly larger than the case gives a plump, over-stuffed appearance). Slip-stitch the fourth side closed. To make a pillowcase with a buttoned opening in back, you'll need one 17"-square piece for the front and two overlapping pieces for the back, each 11¾" by 17".

Double fold and hem along one long side of each of the back pieces, making a ¼"-wide fold and then a 2"-wide fold; press flat. Stitch along the fold lines. Lay the two back pieces right-side up so that their hemmed edges overlap by 2"; pin to hold in place. Using tailor's chalk, mark places for buttonholes 6½" from the top and bottom of the hems; the marks should be 4" apart, and between ½" and 1" from the edge of the top piece, depending on the size of the buttons. Sew buttonholes in the top piece and buttons on the bottom. Pin the two back panels to the front, right sides facing and raw edges aligned. Sew around the perimeter of the pillow. Trim corners, and press seams. Turn case right-side out, and insert a 17"-square pillow. To make a pillow that zips up the back, you'll need two narrower back pieces that meet edge to edge along folded hems. Each back piece should be 9¼" by 17". Press ¾"-wide single-fold hems in one long edge of each piece. Pin and baste so the edges meet; insert a zipper according to manufacturer's instructions.

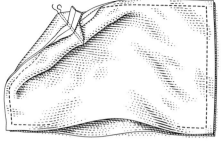

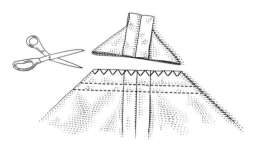

HOW TO MAKE A BOX CUSHION

The pairs of boxy back and arm cushions on page 113 are made from 4 yards of plain canvas, chosen to match the sofa's slipcover. The bed-pillow inserts with which they are stuffed don't need to have special corners; the box-seam corners in the canvas cases shape the feather-and-down fillings. To make the cushions, cut the canvas into four 22½"-by-14½" rectangles and four 38"-by-20" rectangles. Align two of the smaller rectangles; pin and sew ½" seams around the perimeter, leaving a 12" opening centered in one of the long sides, as shown. With your hand inside the pillowcase, open up one corner and realign the fabric so the seam line runs up the center of the corner, bisecting it as shown (top). Measuring along the seam, mark a point 1½" from the tip of the corner. Draw a line through this point, perpendicular to the seam. Sew two rows of stitching along this line, trim off the point of the corner, and serge or sew a zigzag seam along the raw edges (above). Repeat for other three corners. Insert a 23"-by-15" pillow; slip-stitch opening closed. Repeat the process for other pair of small rectangles and for both pairs of large rectangles, inserting 40"-by-21" pillows in the larger cases.

HOW TO MAKE A HARLEQUIN PILLOW

Blocks of elegant, low-key color joined together on the diagonal bring drama to the large silk throw pillow on page 113. The finished pillow cover is 22" square. To make it, you need one 23½" square of taupe silk and one 23½" square of pewter silk. Fold each square on the diagonal, and press; cut along the fold line (below). Fold each of the resulting triangles from corner to corner; press, and cut along the folds. Place one taupe triangle on top of one pewter triangle, right sides facing, and sew a ½" seam along one short side, as shown (bottom, left). Repeat with remaining three pairs of contrasting triangles, always placing the taupe triangle on top of the pewter triangle and sewing along the same short side. Open the pairs of sewn triangles out flat; press seams (bottom, right). Lay one of these two-color triangles on top of another, right sides facing so that alternating triangle colors are on top of one another; sew a ½" seam along the long side. Repeat with the other two triangles. Open flat to create squares, and press seams. Sew the two resulting squares together, right sides facing, along three sides. Turn the pillowcase inside out, and press. Insert a 23" pillow, and slip-stitch it closed.

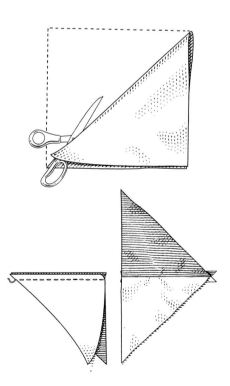

ABOVE A luxurious apple-green cashmere blanket adds a jolt of satisfying color to a traditional Lawson–style sofa and sets off an assortment of textured white pillows. Inexpensive cotton twill tape is woven to make the large square pillowcase; moss fringe edges another. A wide basket-weave upholstery ribbon borders the small boudoir pillow and is repeated at the sofa's hem, where it has been topstitched to the edge of the slipcover. OPPOSITE Touches of navy make a plain white sofa look fresh and tailored. Narrow back pillows emphasize lean contours, formerly obscured by stiff, tall cushions. A canvas throw draped over the back is trimmed in indigo linen, also used as welting on the pillows. A machine-embroidered monogram completes the country-club look.

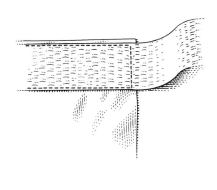

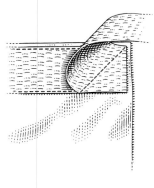

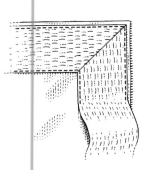

1   2   3

ADDING A BASKET-WEAVE BORDER

The tiny boudoir pillow on page 116 is trimmed in the same basket-weave upholstery tape that edges the sofa's slipcover (right). To make a small pillow with a wide border, cut two rectangles of fine linen, each 13" by 18". Cut 3"-wide basket-weave upholstery tape to a length of 61". Pin the tape to the right side of one of the linen rectangles, ½" in from the raw edges of the fabric. Topstitch along both sides of the tape, about ⅛" from its edges. At the corners, miter the ribbon as shown above. 1 Topstitch a seam perpendicular to the ribbon ½" in from the raw edge of fabric. 2 Fold the ribbon back on itself, and topstitch a seam angling in 45° from the corner. 3 Fold ribbon down so it continues around the perimeter of the fabric. At the last corner, fold the raw end of the ribbon under, at a 45° angle, trimming off any excess; slip-stitch in place by hand. Lay the second piece of linen over the first, right sides facing, and sew around three sides, ½" from the raw edges. Insert a boudoir-size pillow, and slip-stitch the fourth side closed.

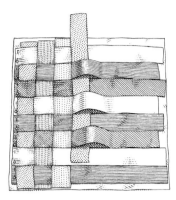

HOW TO MAKE A BASKET-WEAVE PILLOW

Graphic texture brings visual interest to a white-on-white pillow. The 18"-square pillow on page 116 has one side of woven twill tape; the other side is plain muslin. To make it, cut one 19" square of natural-colored cotton muslin and one 21" square of medium-weight woven cotton interfacing (the interfacing will eventually be trimmed to 19"; for now, the extra material makes it easier to weave on). Cut 42' of 1½"-wide cotton twill tape into twenty-four 21" lengths. With the interfacing lying glue-side up, place twelve lengths of tape side by side, pinning them to the interfacing at each end to hold them in place. Weave the other twelve pieces of tape over and under them (above), pushing each row snug against the one before it. Iron tape onto the interfacing, according to manufacturer's directions. Trim 1" from all sides. Lay the muslin square over the woven-tape square, right sides facing. Pin, and stitch around three sides, ½" from raw edges. Clip corners; turn right-side out. Insert an 18"-square pillow. Slip-stitch closed.

HOW TO MAKE A MOSS-FRINGE PILLOW

The easiest way to dress up a simple knife-edge pillow is to sew a length of fringe or other trim directly into the seam. A wide variety of trims are available from sewing-supply stores. Look for one that complements the pillow fabric in color, texture, or fiber, but adds an element of contrast as well. The smoothness of the silk fabric used to make the pillow on page 116 is played up by the fluffy moss fringe that frames it. To make this pillow, cut a length of champagne silk into two rectangles, each 18½" by 12½". Pin a 62" length of moss fringe to perimeter of one of the silk rectangles, with the right side of the fabric up and the fringe facing inward. Clip notches into the fringe tape where it rounds the corners so that it lies flat. Overlap the two ends of the tape, bringing their raw ends out past the edge of the fabric; pin. Stitch the tape to the fabric, sewing ½" in from the raw edges. Lay the second rectangle over this piece, right sides facing, and pin. Stitch around three sides. Trim corners, turn right-side out, and press. Insert a custom-made feather-and-down pillow (see the Guide), and slip-stitch the case closed.

HOW TO MAKE A CANVAS THROW

Not all throw blankets need to be warm and cozy. A canvas throw edged in linen has a crisp, clean feeling that suits summertime interiors. The throw on page 117 is made of a single layer of navy-blue cotton canvas edged with a 2¼" band of indigo linen. Smoothed over the back of the sofa, it acts as a backdrop to bright-white pillows. This throw blanket is not meant to be reversible; the trim shows up on only one side. Begin by cutting the canvas into a 57"-by-72" rectangle. Cut linen into four 3¼"-wide bands—two 56" long, and two 73" long. Pin the linen bands to all four edges of the canvas so that the right side of the linen faces the back side of the canvas and the edges are flush. Stitch around the perimeter of the canvas, ½" from raw edges. Fold the linen to the front side of the canvas; turn under a ½" hem in the raw edge of the linen (right), and press flat. Topstitch the linen to the canvas ⅛" from this fold, as shown. At corners, where two linen bands overlap, sew the bottom one straight out to edge. Trim excess. Fold the second one to a 45° angle, and slip-stitch it over the top of the first.

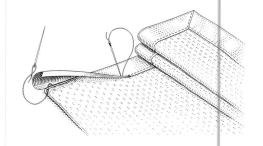

HOW TO MAKE WELTED PILLOWS

Adding high-contrast trim to plain white back pillows turns them from soft objects into sharply outlined shapes. The pillowcases on page 117 are made from cotton canvas, in a shade of white carefully chosen to match the sofa's slipcover. Their indigo welting is made from the same linen used to trim the canvas throw (opposite). If you intend to wash the finished pillowcases, be sure to wash the welting several times before you sew, so its dye doesn't bleed into the white fabric. Cut the white canvas into six rectangles, each 27" by 17½". Have a 5½"-by-6" monogram embroidered onto one rectangle (this can be done by custom embroiderers; see the Guide). To make welting for one pillow, cut the indigo linen on the bias into 2"-wide strips. Sew the strips end to end to make an 89" length. Fold the strip, right-side out, with raw edges even, around an 89" length of ¼" cotton cording. Using the zipper foot on your sewing machine, stitch along the length of the strip as close to the cording as possible to ensure a snug fit (right).

Trim raw edges to ½" from the seam. Pin the welting to the right side of one of the canvas rectangles, with the welting facing toward the center and the raw edges flush. Clip notches into the seams where the welting rounds the corners so it lies flat. Overlap ends. Stitch in place, following the seam line on the welting. Lay a second rectangle over this piece, right sides facing, and pin. Stitch around the three sides. Trim corners, turn right-side out, and press. Insert a custom-made feather-and-down pillow (see the Guide), or use a queen-size bed pillow, which will be slightly large for the case, giving the cushion an over-stuffed look. Slip-stitch the fourth side closed.

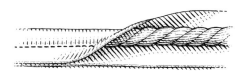

THIS PAGE A traditional English–style sofa, with low-slung arms and a leisurely lean to its back, appears more graceful when the back cushions are replaced by one long bolster. The jacquard case adds visual interest to the plain upholstery while preserving the room's calm mood. Fawn-colored velvet ribbon trims the pillow and the slipcover's hem. The Art Deco nesting tables are German; the lamp is a pottery jar topped with a brown-paper shade.

The pillow on the opposite page has a leaf-patterned jacquard cotton front and an off-white canvas back. Before sewing, the canvas was dyed in tea; any ordinary tea can be used. Cut the fabric 4" larger than you'll need for the bolster, in case it shrinks. Hand wash it gently in mild soap; rinse well. Keep the fabric wet while you prepare the tea bath. You'll need a pot large enough for the fabric to move around in without being cramped. Fill the pot with water, and bring to a boil. Steep the tea; use 8 to 12 bags for every yard of fabric, depending on how dark you want the canvas to be. Add ½ cup of salt per yard, as a bonding agent. Remove the tea bags, and transfer the wet, unfolded fabric to the tea bath, stirring constantly while on the stove to ensure that the dye takes evenly. Gradually raise the temperature until the tea just boils. Turn off the heat, and let the fabric soak for about 30 minutes, stirring constantly. Rinse until the water runs clear. Hang on a clothesline to dry, attaching one edge of the fabric with clothespins; don't drape over the line, or the fold will show. To make the bolster, cut each fabric into a rectangle 72" by 18". Cut 2"-wide velvet ribbon into four 73" lengths and four 19" lengths. Lay the ribbon right-side up around the perimeter of both rectangles, ½" in from edges of fabric, folding one ribbon end around the other at the corners to create a neat finish. Pin and topstitch the ribbon in place, sewing as close as possible to the edge of the ribbon with matching thread. To make the welting for the pillow, cut the canvas on the bias into 2"-wide strips. Sew the strips end to end to make a 181" length. Fold the strip, right-side out, with raw edges even around a 181" length of ¼" cotton cording. Using the zipper foot on your sewing machine, stitch along the length of the strip as close to the cording as possible to ensure a snug fit (see drawing on page 121). Trim raw edges to ½" from seam. Pin the welting to the right side of one of the ribbon-trimmed rectangles, aligning the seam in the welting with the seam in the velvet, with the welting facing toward the center of the rectangle. Clip notches into the seams where the welting rounds the corners so it lies flat. Overlap the two ends of the welting, bringing their raw ends out past the edge of the fabric; pin. Stitch in place, following the seam line on the welting. Pin the canvas rectangle over this piece, right sides facing and raw edges aligned. Stitch together, just to the inside of the seam line on the jacquard piece. Insert a custom-made feather-and-down pillow (see the Guide), and slip-stitch the fourth side closed.

ABOVE A silver-leafed daybed doubles as a sofa in the living room of a summer cottage. Piled with an assortment of pillows, the daybed becomes a versatile spot for talking, napping, or settling down for the night. The pillowcases and mattress cover are all sewn from brightly colored linen, a fabric that has natural cooling properties. A wool throw wards off evening chills. OPPOSITE On a front porch, a sofa outfitted like a daybed is the perfect place to camp out on a sunny morning and read the newspaper. Plenty of pillows are on hand to rearrange as needed for sitting or dozing. Their cases are made from a variety of new and vintage fabrics, including striped mattress ticking and linen tea towels. Echoing the bright red, a bunch of anemones sits on a forest-green coffee table whose top was custom-finished with galvanized steel. One large linen slipcover encases both seat cushions; the same fabric covers the cushions on the wicker chairs.

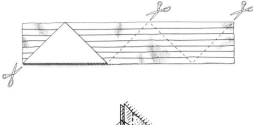

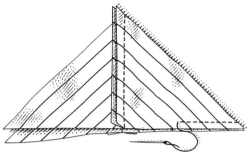

HOW TO MAKE A STRIPED PILLOW

The striped pillow on page 124, pieced together on the diagonal, is similar to the silk pillow on page 113 (instructions on page 115), with one important difference: Matching up the stripes requires great precision when measuring, cutting, and sewing the fabric. It helps to use a template when cutting out the pieces and to leave extra-wide seam allowances on all sides, so that you have some leeway if you need to make adjustments once the pieces have been cut. To make the pillow, cut a 20" square from craft paper; draw diagonals from corner to corner; cut along the diagonal, and use only one of the resulting triangles as a template. Lay it on a piece of striped linen, aligning the base of the triangle with a stripe. Trace around perimeter, and move template over 20". Repeat to create a total of four linen triangles, and cut them out (top). Cut out an 18" square for the back of the pillow. Align two of the triangles, right sides facing, so that stripes meet up exactly. Pin, and sew along one short side, leaving 1" seam allowance. Repeat with other two triangles. Open, and press flat (above). Align these two triangles with right sides facing, so that stripes meet. Pin, and sew long side, 1" from raw edges, to create square. Unfold, and press flat. Lay this square facedown over back square. Sew up three sides. Insert a pillow, and slip-stitch closed.

A daybed shouldn't always look like someone just slept there. A simple slipcover dresses it up for its 9-to-5 job. The daybed on page 124 is covered in an easy-to-make case of celery-green linen. To make it, first measure the length and width of the mattress. Add half the thickness of mattress to measurements, plus 1" seam allowance. Cut two panels of fabric to this dimension. Align the panels, with right sides facing, and sew around the perimeter, beginning and ending approximately 18" from the corners on one long side, to create a gap where you can insert the mattress. While the case is still inside out, square off each corner as follows: Place your hand inside the slipcover, open up one corner, and realign the fabric so the seam line runs up the center of the corner, bisecting it as shown in the drawing on page 115. Holding a ruler perpendicular to the seam, find the point where the width of the corner, from edge to edge, is equal to the thickness of the mattress. Draw a line through this point, perpendicular to the seam. Sew two rows of stitching along this line, and trim off the point of the corner (below); then serge or sew a zigzag seam along the raw edges. Repeat for other three corners. Sew a zigzag seam along the raw edges at the opening in the fourth side of the cover. Insert the mattress, and slip-stitch closed.

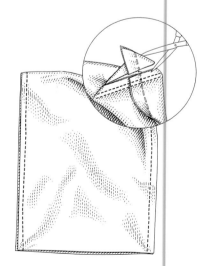

HOW TO MAKE A BOLSTER COVER

Bolsters cushion the ends of a daybed, making it a more versatile and accommodating seat. Firm and solid, they can serve as back supports or armrests. The easiest way to cover a bolster is with a simple sleeve of fabric, cinched with drawstrings at each end. The bolster cover shown above and on page 124 is made from a 46"-by-22" rectangle of blue linen. Sew a zigzag stitch all around the perimeter of the fabric to prevent unraveling. Double fold a hem along both short sides, making a ¼"-wide fold, then a 1½"-wide fold at each end; press flat. Topstitch the hem over the double fold. Attach a 24" length of blue cotton cord to a safety pin, and thread it through the seam tunnel, pinning the other end in place to keep it from being pulled into the tunnel. Repeat on the other side. (You can also make a cord from the same fabric used to cover the bolster.) Cut two pieces, each 24" long and 1½" wide. Fold one in half lengthwise, right sides facing, so that raw edges

meet, and pin. Sew, ½" from raw edges, along the long side and up one of the short sides. Use a dowel to push the sewn end back through the cord, and turn the whole thing right-side out. Press flat. Fold the raw edges at the remaining end inward, and slip-stitch shut. Thread the finished cord through the tunnel in the fabric as described above. To form the sleeve, fold the rectangle in half, right-side in, and sew the long sides together, ½" from the edge, leaving 2" unsewn at each end. Turn right-side out. Insert the bolster. To cover the exposed ends of the pillow, cut circles of linen the size of the bolster's ends. Zigzag stitch around the circumference to prevent unraveling. Lay circles onto ends of bolster inserts, and tack in place with a few stitches around the rim. Slip large glass beads onto the ends of the cords to keep them from slipping into the tunnels; secure with knots above and below the beads. Pull drawstrings taut, and tie.

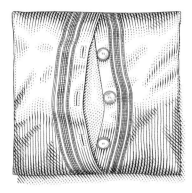

HOW TO MAKE A BUTTONED PILLOW

Vintage household linens, such as tea and hand towels, can have wonderful second lives as pillowcases. The fabric is often softened by use or polished from repeated ironing. Because many of these linens come in odd sizes, you may need to have a pillow insert custom made. (See the Guide for sources, or contact an upholsterer in your area to find out who supplies his pillows.) The dark ecru and red striped pillow on page 125 began as an ordinary tea towel, 15" wide by 28" long. To make this pillowcase, lay a towel right-side up, and fold the two narrow ends toward the center so that they overlap by 1". Sew three buttonholes into the overlapping layer, ½" in from the edge, and 5½", 10", and 14½", respectively, from the top of the pillowcase (above). Sew three buttons into the under-lapping layer, aligning them with the buttonholes. Button the buttons, and turn the towel inside out, so that the buttons are centered on one side. Sew along the top and bottom edges, with a ½" seam allowance. Turn right-side out, and press. Unbutton, insert a 14"-by-13" pillow, and close.

Vintage toweling isn't quite the same thing as towels. Woven in long, narrow bolts, toweling is fabric that was meant to be cut into short pieces at a dry-goods store, then hemmed at home before being put to use drying dishes or hands. It often turns up at vintage clothing and textile stores and at flea markets. Because it already has selvages along the sides, hems can be kept to a minimum, and it's easy to work with. One of the pillowcases on the sofa on page 125 (see opposite for detail) is made from toweling that's been sewn into a sleeve and simply tied closed at the sides. To make it, fold a 35" length of toweling in half so the ends meet and the right side faces inward. Sew a seam ½" from the raw edges; finish the edges with a zigzag stitch to prevent unraveling. Attach 12" lengths of cotton tape to the front and back of the sleeve, halfway along each side, sewing them to the inside of the sleeve with small Xs of stitches to secure. Next, cover a 17"-square pillow insert with contrasting fabric; we used natural linen. Cut two 17" squares of fabric. Pin the squares together, right sides facing with raw edges aligned. Sew the fabric along three sides, ½" from the edges. Turn right-side out, and press. Slip-stitch the fourth side closed by hand. Insert the pillow; tie closed.

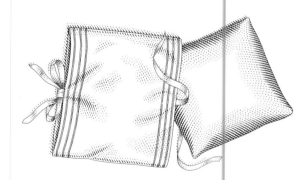

HOW TO MAKE A ROLL PILLOW

A bolster made of vintage mattress ticking (above) nestles in the corner of the porch sofa on page 125. Ticking, available at flea markets and vintage-textile stores, is often striped, but its pattern isn't the only thing that distinguishes it from other fabrics. In the days when bedding was commonly filled with feathers or horsehair, ticking's dense, multilayered weave prevented stuffings from poking through. Today, this thickly woven fabric is no longer manufactured, and vintage remnants can be quite expensive. If you have old pillows and mattresses whose stuffings have disintegrated, consider reusing their ticking cases if they are in good shape. Otherwise, any striped fabric will do. To make the bolster shown, which is 33" long and approximately 6" in diameter, you'll need a rectangle of fabric, 34" by 15", with the ticking stripes running parallel to the short sides; and two circles, each 6" in diameter. Cut fabric to these dimensions. Baste along the short sides of the rectangle, ½" from the raw edges. With the right sides facing inward, pin the long sides of the rectangle together to make a sleeve. Beginning at one end, sew a seam ½" from raw edges; sew 11", leave an 11" gap, then sew the remaining 11" to the other end. At one end of the sleeve, pull the basting thread to gather the fabric; pin to the perimeter of the circle, right sides facing inward, as shown. Space the gathers evenly, and stitch in place with seams ½" from raw edges. Remove the basting. Repeat at the other end of the sleeve. Turn right-side out, and press. Insert a bolster pillow, and sew up the gap using slip stitches.

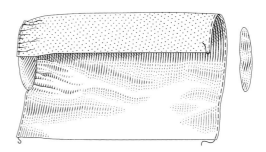

ABOVE A quick cure for the dog days: Linen pillowcases in ripe shades of watermelon and tangerine revive a tired bed. Simple to make, they have tremendous impact; you needn't change another thing to usher this room into summer. A shaped linen cover slipped over the headboard keeps the room feeling quiet and cool. An antique French bistro table serves as a nightstand. The windowsill catches the table's overflow: a nineteenth-century drawing of a tulip, a family photo, and a dish of beachcombing finds. OPPOSITE A pair of linen coverlets brings a shock of exotic color to a guest bedroom, making the snow-white sheets and button-hem pillowcases look even fresher than usual. The borders are edged with orchid piping weighted with buckshot cord to pull the fabric flat and smooth. Though heavy, these spreads are cool against the skin, since linen's fibers wick away heat and moisture. Fish drawings swim across the beaded-board walls. A tiny, flat metal alarm clock sits beside a collection of polished stones. The lamp is topped with a paper shade painted with high-gloss oil-based paint and edged with self-adhesive aluminum tape. A small vase of dill flowers sits on the windowsill.

A fabric cover refinishes an old wooden headboard without requiring any scraping, sanding, or painting. The heavy-weight fabric works like instant upholstery, softening and padding the lines of the wooden form underneath it; thinner fabrics would be too flimsy for this project. The headboard cover shown on page 130 is made from ecru basket-weave linen. First, wash the fabric to preshrink it. Lay the headboard flat on a piece of craft paper. Trace around the outline, then set the headboard aside. Add 2" all around the perimeter (more if the headboard is especially thick), and cut out template. Pin the paper pattern carefully to a double layer of ecru linen, aligning the bottom edge of the pattern with the linen's selvaged edges, and cut out the linen. With right sides facing, sew the two pieces of linen together, with ½" seam allowances, beginning 24" from bottom corner on one side, and stopping 24" from bottom corner on the other. Fold back seam allowances along these 24"-long slits, and press. Cut four 26" lengths of 1½"-wide cotton tape. Pin along slits so that the edge of the tape aligns with the fold and covers the raw edge of the fabric. Tuck the top and bottom of the tape under by ½", and topstitch around the perimeter of the tape (below). Make six evenly spaced grommet holes along all four slits. Cut two 60" lengths of linen ribbon; lace one through each set of grommet holes. Slip the cover over the headboard, and tighten the laces.

HOW TO MAKE A PILLOWCASE

Bright linen pillowcases with contrasting hems are all it takes to energize a quiet bedroom for summertime. Before sewing, prewash all fabrics to test for bleeding and to allow them to shrink. The watermelon-and-tangerine pillowcases on page 130, which fit standard-size pillows, require a 24"-by-40" piece of watermelon linen and an 11"-by-40" strip of tangerine linen. Place tangerine fabric atop watermelon fabric, right sides facing, aligning fabrics along the 40" edges. Sew together along this side, ½" from the raw edge. Open up fabric, and press hem against tangerine fabric. Sew a zigzag seam along the raw 40" edge of tangerine fabric. Fold the piece in half crosswise, right sides facing; leaving the tangerine end unsewn, sew along the two sides. Fold the tangerine cuff so that its zigzagged edge overlaps by ½" the seam joining the two pieces. Press. Turn the pillowcase right-side out, and stitch in the seam—that is, sew on the outside where the fabrics meet—in order to secure the cuff.

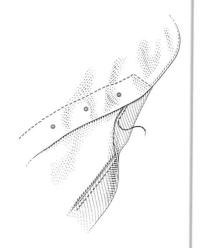

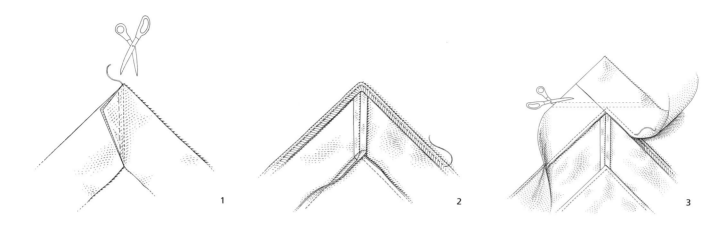

A pair of linen coverlets for two single beds makes the most of the fiber's unique characteristics. Linen is extremely strong and heavy, due to the density of its fibers. But it's cooler than other natural fabrics because of the alignment of its long, straight cells, which create avenues that allow moisture to pass through easily and evaporate quickly, keeping skin cool and dry on hot summer nights. Before starting to make these coverlets, please note that this is an advanced project meant for experienced sewers. To make the orange-and-green coverlet shown on page 131, you'll need a piece of 46"-by-83" orange linen; two panels of 11"-by-103" lime-green linen and two panels of 11"-by-67" lime-green linen for the top border; and two panels of 11"-by-123" lime-green linen and two panels of 11"-by-87" lime-green linen for the underside border. The pink coverlet with orange borders is made with the same measurements. To make the top border, begin by aligning at one end one short and one long green panel, right sides facing. Draw a 45° diagonal line from one corner to the other side; sew along this line. 1 Trim away the excess fabric; press the seam flat. Repeat this process at three more corners, using one other long and one other short green panel to create a continuous rectangular green border. Join this border to the perimeter of the orange panel, laying one side of the green border at a time over the orange panel, with raw edges aligned and right sides facing. Sew ½" from raw edges, clipping the seam allowance at the corners so that the border lies flat. 2 Press the seam

allowance outward, toward the green panels. To make the welting: Cut orchid-pink linen on the bias into strips 1½" wide. Sew strips end to end to create a 340" (28⅓') length. Press all seams. Wrap this strip right-side out, with raw edges even, around a 340"-long strand of buckshot weights (see the Guide). Using the zipper-foot attachment on your sewing machine, sew the length of the strip to encase the buckshot. Trim to ½" from stitch line. Pin the welting to the outside perimeter of the green border so that buckshot faces inward and the raw edges meet, clipping the seam allowance at the corners so the welting lies flat. Sew the welting in place, ½" in from the raw edge. Lay the remaining four green panels around the perimeter of the coverlet, right sides facing, so that the raw edges meet and the welting is covered. Pin and sew ½" from raw edges. Unfold these panels. 3 Draw a line at each corner on these new panels, perpendicular to the mitered corner seams in the first set of green panels; then add a ½" seam allowance, and cut off corner. Flip the four new panels to the back side of the coverlet. Fold under the seam allowance on the mitered corners of the panels; press. Slip-stitch by hand. Pin the loose lower edge of the green panels in place so they lie flat, and cover the back side of the seam where the orange panel meets the green border. Turn the coverlet right-side up, and gutter-stitch in the seam where the orange and green meet, stitching through both layers to secure the back border in place, and trim the seam allowance.

TRIMMING A BLANKET

A contrasting hem visually frames a blanket and also gives it a soft, smooth edge to tuck under your chin on a cold winter night. To make one of the blankets shown above, start with a piece of soft wool fabric the dimensions that you want your finished blanket to be. To trim it in ribbon, you'll need satin ribbon that's at least 4" wide and 4" longer than the perimeter of the blanket, cut into four pieces, each 1" longer than the side of the blanket to which it will be sewn. To trim it in contrasting wool, you need to cut wool into four strips, each 5" wide and 1" longer than the side of the blanket; the extra width is for a hem, since the wool doesn't have a natural selvage the way ribbon does. Turn and press ½" under both long edges of each wool strip. Mark the width of the hem at both ends of the blanket with chalk lines. Flip the blanket over, and repeat on the other side. Lay one hem strip or length of ribbon on the blanket (with the pressed edges down, for wool) so that one edge lines up with the chalk line, and the strip or ribbon extends ½" past the blanket at each end. Pin. Turn, and press the excess at each end flush with the blanket edges. Fold the strip or ribbon over the blanket edge to the other side so that it meets the second chalk line. Pin, making sure that the hem is the same width on both sides of the blanket. Topstitch through all three layers, about ¼" from the hem line.

HOW TO MAKE A DOUBLE-FACED BLANKET

Double-faced wools—two layers that are held together by a web of threads—are available at most fabric stores. They can be used to make blankets that are especially warm, and the contrasting colors give character to a quiet bed. To make the blanket on the opposite page, start with a piece of double-faced wool 1" longer and wider than the dimensions you want the finished blanket to be. To make rounded corners, cut out a paper circle that is 4" in diameter for a pattern, or use a lid or saucer the same size. Lay the circle on the blanket at a corner so that it just meets adjacent edges. Pin and trace the arc of the circle's circumference where it fits inside the corner with tailor's chalk. Cut along this line. Using a seam ripper, carefully separate the two faces of the fabric 1" all around; they should come apart surprisingly easily, revealing a shared set of threads in between (below). Fold the raw edges ½" inward, clipping the corners as necessary to make the fabric lie flat. Line up the folded edges evenly, and pin them together. Thread the sewing machine so that the top and bottom bobbin colors correspond to the top and bottom fabric colors. Carefully stitch around the perimeter of the blanket, ¼" in from the folded edges.

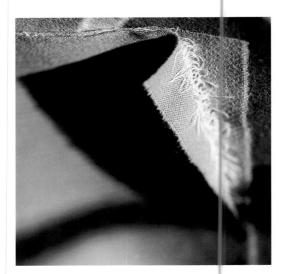

THIS PAGE A warm wool blanket coupled with cool cotton sheets promises a good night's sleep in a single alcove bed tucked up under the eaves of a nineteenth-century farmhouse. Double-faced wool is as thick as two blankets, but more manageable; it is easily converted with elegantly finished borders.

The Guide

Items pictured but not listed are from private collections. Addresses and telephone numbers of sources may change prior to or following publication, as may price and availability of any item.

COVER
SWEATER by TSE Cashmere. PANTS by Prada. MARTHA STEWART EVERYDAY COLORS PAINT in "Chalk" (G32) on trim, "Wintersurf" (G23) on wall, and "Viburnum" (A20) on ceiling, available at Kmart; 800-866-0086 for store locations.

PICTURES

page 10
10'-by-14' MARASH RUG, $7,895, from ABC Carpet & Home, 888 Broadway, New York, NY 10003; 212-473-3000. FAIRHILL SOFA, $8,080, from George Smith, 73 Spring Street, New York, NY 10012; 212-226-4747. TELEPHONE TABLE, $1,500, from Mariette Himes Gomez Associates, 506 East 74th Street, New York, NY 10021; 212-288-6856. Empire SIDE TABLE and Louis XV ARMCHAIRS from Pierre Deux Antiques, 369 Bleecker Street, New York, NY 10014; 212-243-7740. NESTING TABLES from Malmaison Antiques, 253 East 74th Street, New York, NY 10021; 212-288-7569. CASHMERE THROW, $1,050, from Frette, 799 Madison Avenue, New York, NY 10021; 212-988-5221. CAMEO PLAQUE, $1,650, from Yale Burge Antiques, 315 East 62nd Street, New York, NY 10021;

212-838-4005. Nancy Lorenz black silk PAINTING SERIES, $500 each, from AERO, 132 Spring Street, New York, NY 10012; 212-966-1500. 1950s INK DRAWING, MASK WATERCOLOR, and LANDSCAPE PAINTING, all from Alan Moss, 436 Lafayette Street, New York, NY 10003; 212-473-1310. HORTICULTURAL PRINT and ARCHITECTURAL WATERCOLORS, $600 to $1,500, from Sentimento, 306 East 61st Street, New York, NY 10021; 212-750-3111. To the trade only. 22-karat-gold Regency WALL BRACKET, $1,050, from Holly Hunt, 979 Third Avenue, New York, NY 10022; 212-755-6555.

page 11
French GALLERY RODS, $11 to $25, from New York Central Framing, 102 Third Avenue, New York, NY 10003; 212-420-6060. French STOOL from Mariette Himes Gomez Associates, see above.

page 12
MATISSE SKETCH, $1,650, from Nancy Corzine, 979 Third Avenue, #8, New York, NY 10022; 212-223-8340. To the trade only. ARCHITECTURAL WATER-COLORS, $600 to $1,500, from Sentimento, see above. Swedish PAINTED CHAIR, $1,425, from David Barrett, 131 East 71st Street, New York, NY 10021; 212-585-3180. LINEN PILLOW, $350,

from Mariette Himes Gomez Associates, see above.

page 13
Antique SLIPPER CHAIR, $3,000, from Mariette Himes Gomez Associates, see above.

page 14
Custom SILVER-LEAFED FRAMES and large WALNUT FRAME from Skyframe & Art, Inc., 96 Spring Street, New York, NY 10012; 212-925-7856.

page 15
SWEDISH DESK, $2,775, from David Barrett, see above. ANTIQUE MAP, $2,500, from W. Graham Arader III, 29 East 72nd Street, New York, NY 10021; 212-628-3668. BUTTERFLY ENGRAVING, $285, from Ursus Prints, 981 Madison Avenue, New York, NY 10021; 212-772-8787. Custom SHADOW BOX from Skyframe & Art, Inc., see above. BUTTERFLY, $39, from Maxilla & Mandible, Ltd., 451 Columbus Avenue, New York, NY 10024; 212-724-6173. 1795 FRENCH CHAIR, $2,125, from Sentimento, see above. Assorted FRAMED PRINTS from Winter Works on Paper, 160 Fifth Avenue, No. 178, New York, NY 10011; 212-352-9013. By appointment only.

page 18
8"-by-10" PICTURE FRAMES, $8.60 each, from New York Central Framing, see above. ASHLEY SOFA, $8,870, from George Smith, see above.

CASHMERE BLANKET, $480, from Salon Moderne, 281 Lafayette Street, New York, NY 10011; 212-219-3439. Silk MATTRESS PILLOWS, $350 each, from AERO, see above.

page 19
Sepia HORTICULTURAL PRINTS, $800 each, from Reymer-Jourdan Antiques, 29 East 10th Street, New York, NY 10003; 212-674-4470.

page 20
1930s white NESTING TABLE from AERO, see above. Mahogany French DAYBED, $7,500, from Mariette Himes Gomez Associates, see above. PHOTO-GRAVURES, $150 each, from Winter Works on Paper, see above. Custom FRAMES, from Sky Frame & Art, Inc., see above.

page 22
BOTANICAL PRINT, from Winter Works on Paper, see above.

page 23
1860s English MIRROR FRAME by Watts, $1,200, from Gill & Lagodich Fine Period Frame Gallery, 108 Reade Street, New York, NY 10013; 212-619-0631. Nineteenth-century upholstered English SIDE CHAIR from A. Smith Antiques, Ltd., 235 East 60th Street, New York, NY 10022; 212-888-6337. SATIN RIBBONS, $6.50 to $10 per yard, from Hyman Hendler & Sons, 67 West 38th Street, New York, NY 10018; 212-840-8393. Assorted FRAMES from C.I.T.E. Design,

100 Wooster Street, New York, NY 10012; 212-431-7272. EDWARD TRAVIES WATERCOLOR from W. Graham Arader III, 29 East 72nd Street, New York, NY 10021; 212-628-3668.

pages 24 and 25
MARTHA STEWART EVERYDAY COLORS PAINT in "Goose Down" (F09), "Conch" (G24), "Wei-maraner" (G15), "Coir" (G19), "Adobe" (G13), and "Homespun" (H03), available at Kmart; 800-866-0086 for store locations. 3½"-by-5" BEVELED FRAMES, $12 each, from Pearl Paint Frames, 56 Lispenard Street, New York, NY 10013; 212-226-6966. NICKEL HINGES from Simon's Hardware & Bath, 421 Third Avenue, New York, NY 10016; 212-532-9220. Dennis Daniels FRAMES, $6.40 to $8.40, from Sam Flax, 425 Park Avenue, New York, NY 10022; 212-620-3060.

pages 26 and 27
Custom SHADOW BOXES available from: Gallery Frames/Archival Framing, 418 Broome Street, 2nd Floor, New York, NY 10013; 212-226-7430. Eric Walton/Icon Design Studio, 338 West 49th Street, New York, NY 10019; 212-581-8529. Drummond Framing, 27 East 21st Street, New York, NY 10010; 212-254-5033.

page 27
SPECIMEN INSECTS from Evolution, 120 Spring Street, New York, NY 10012; 212-343-1114.

TABLES & STOOLS

page 30
CHENILLE FABRIC on large footstool, $57 per yard, and SILK FABRIC on smaller footstool, $33 per yard, both from ABC Carpet & Home, 888 Broadway, New York, NY 10003; 212-473-3000. Bronze TASHINIMA RUG from Odegard, 200 Lexington Avenue, Suite 1206, New York, NY 10016; 212-545-0069.

page 31
WOODEN TOOLBOX, $125, from Sammy's, 484 Broome Street, New York, NY 10013; 212-343-2357. 1⅜" wood or metal CURTAIN FINIALS, $7 to $20 per pair, from Bed Bath & Beyond, 620 Sixth Avenue, New York, NY 10011; 212-255-3550. Brushed nickel bin PULL HANDLES, $4.50 to $5.50 each, from Restoration Hardware, 15 Coch Road, Corte Madera, CA 94925; 415-945-3448 or 800-762-1005. ⅜" GROSGRAIN RIBBON, $1.60 per yard, from Hyman Hendler & Sons, 67 West 38th Street, New York, NY 10018; 212-840-8393. LINEN FABRIC, $19.95 per yard, from Rosen & Chadick, 246 West 40th Street, New York, NY 10018; 212-869-0142. MARTHA STEWART EVERYDAY COLORS PAINT on wooden toolbox in "Goose Down" (F09), available at Kmart; 800-866-0086 for store locations. "Kjaerholm" glass SOFA TABLE (#320-61), $3,990, from ICF Group, 305 East 63rd Street, New York, NY 10021; 212-750-0900. TAN PILLOW, $395, from AERO, 132 Spring Street, New York, NY 10012; 212-966-1500. JADE BOWL, $130, from Global Table, 107-109 Sullivan Street, New York, NY 10012; 212-431-5839.

page 33
WOODEN FOOTSTOOLS, $2,250 for pair, from Pierre Deux Antiques, 369 Bleecker Street, New York, NY 10014; 212-243-7740. Irish LINEN FABRIC, $24 per yard, and MOSS FRINGE, $8 per yard, from ABC Carpet & Home, see above. Custom FEATHER-AND-DOWN PILLOWS, from Allied Down, 84 Oak Street, Brooklyn, NY 11222; 718-389-5454. ⅝" French GROSGRAIN RIBBON, $2 per yard, from Hyman Hendler & Sons, see above.

page 34
Black UPHOLSTERY BACKING, $5 per yard, from BZI Distributors,

105 Eldridge Street, New York, NY 10002; 212-966-6690.

page 36
Weathered Victorian DRESSER MIRROR, $450; French miniature DRESSMAKER'S MOLD, $225; granite ART DECO CLOCK, $125; Abercrombie & Fitch PEWTER FLASKS, $130 for pair; PEWTER VASE, $70; paneled FARMHOUSE CUPBOARD, $575; 1920s MILK-GLASS VASES, $125 for pair; nineteenth- and twentieth-century white POTTERY VASES, $65 to $150 each; sailboat shadow-box DIORAMA in gilded box frame, $1,400; Cut-down 1910 PINE FARM TABLE, $400; gilded braided-wood BASKET with tin insert, filled with giant seashells, $225; 1930s OAK OFFICE CHAIRS, $75 to $250 each; VINTAGE-FABRIC PILLOWS, $65 each; all from Ruby Beets Antiques, 1703 Montauk Highway, Bridge-hampton, NY; or P.O. Box 596, Wainscott, NY 11975; 516-537-2802. GALVANIZED-IRON TABLETOP custom-made by Fred Klatt, Hans Klatt & Son, Inc., P.O. Box 156, South Jamesport, NY 11970; 516-722-3515. Office chair SEAT CUSHIONS sewn by Debbie Francis, Debbie's Sewing, 104 Denise Street, Sag Harbor, NY 11963; 516-725-4544. WINDOW SHADES custom-made by Ann Baderian; 718-359-0309. By appointment only. Aubusson NEEDLEPOINT RUG, $5,595, from ABC Carpet & Home, see above.

page 37
Cut-down FARM TABLE, $125, from Ruby Beets Antiques, see above. Custom-made PLATE-GLASS and MILK-GLASS TABLE-TOPS from Glaaass, 152 West 26th Street, New York, NY 10001; 212-463-8000. Mediterranean-stripe COTTON FABRIC, $32 per yard, from Ralph Lauren Home Collection, 1185 Sixth Avenue, New York, NY 10036; 212-642-8700. Oversize PORCELAIN DISH, $85, from Wolfman-Gold and Good Company, 117 Mercer

Street, New York, NY 10012; 212-431-1888. TALL STOOL, $1,200, from Rooms & Gardens, 290 Lafayette Street, New York, NY 10012; 212-431-1297. MARTHA STEWART EVERYDAY COLORS PAINT in "Mercury Glass" (G31), available at Kmart, see above. 54" COTTON TICKING in "Empire One/Olive" by Ian Menkin, $44 per yard, from Coconut Company, 131 Greene Street, New York, NY 10012; 212-539-1940. 1940s DRESSING STOOL from David Stypmann Co., 192 Sixth Avenue, New York, NY 10013; 212-226-5717.

page 38
BENJAMIN MOORE PORCH AND FLOOR PAINT, 800-826-2623 for nearest retailer. Niermann-Weeks "Regence" SLIPPER CHAIR from John Rosselli International, 523 East 73rd Street, New York, NY 10021; 212-772-2137. To the trade only. English inlay ARM-CHAIR with walnut finish, $2,065, from Nancy Corzine, 305 East 63rd Street, New York, NY 10021; 212-758-4240. To the trade only. Circa 1700 Jacobean English oak TAVERN TABLE from Bilhuber, Inc., 330 East 59th Street, New York, NY 10022; 212-308-4888. Marble finial LAMP, $1,200, from Rooms & Gardens, see above. Cloverleaf PEDESTAL TABLE in Macassar ebony veneer, $3,720, from Rose Tarlow-Melrose House at Holly Hunt New York, 979 Third Avenue, New York, NY 10022; 212-755-6555. SILK SATIN on pillows, $80 per yard, from B&J Fabrics, 263 West 40th Street, New York, NY 10018; 212-354-8150.

page 39
WOOL THROW, $125, and Stephen Schermeyer ROPE BENCH, $650, from Ad Hoc, 410 West Broad-way, New York, NY 10012; 212-925-2652. 15" square sycamore PLATTER, $100, from Calvin Klein Home; 800-294-7978 for nearest retailer. Hand-colored FRAMED PHOTOGRAPH and

antique MIRROR from Paula Rubenstein Limited, 65 Prince Street, New York, NY 10012; 212-966-8954. 1920s GATELEG SIDE TABLE from David Stypmann Co., see above. Silver-leafed DAYBED, $1,900, from Claiborne Gallery, 212-475-3072. By appointment only.

page 41
Natural LINEN THROW, $120, from Ad Hoc, see above. Cast-plaster ANTIQUE HEADS, $175 each, and CAST-IRON TABLE, $475, all from Ruby Beets Antiques, see above. Custom-made FROSTED-GLASS TABLETOP from Glaaass, see above.

pages 42 and 43
Circa 1950s WIRE MESH CHAIRS, $450 for set of four, from Paula Rubenstein Limited, see above. 8½'-by-8½' SPLIT-BAMBOO MAT, $375, and large hand-thrown BOWL by Peter Lane, $600, from Stone Road, Montauk Highway and Wainscott Road, Wainscott, NY 11975; 516-537-5656. Green iron EMPIRE CHAIR, $650, from Florentine Craftsmen, 46-24 28th Street, Long Island City, NY 11101; 718-937-7632 or 800-876-3567. Catalog $5. Green PRATT & LAMBERT PAINT (#1611) on chair; 800-289-7728 for nearest retailer. GLASSES, $15, and METAL BUCKET, $22, from Ad Hoc, see above. "Popsicle" LINEN/COTTON FABRIC on pillows, $48 per yard, from Rogers & Goffigon, see above. Custom IRON TABLES, $125 for small and $450 for large, from Morgik, 20 West 22nd Street, New York, NY 10010; 212-463-0304. Pale blue-green oil-base enamel BENJAMIN MOORE PAINT (#451); 800-826-2623 for nearest retailer. GLASS MOSAIC TILES by Vetricolor, $7.35 to $24 per square foot, available from Nemo Tile Company, 48 East 21st Street, New York, NY 10010; 212-505-0009. 32"-by-32" custom PLASTER TABLETOP, $1,200, by Art in Construction, 34 West

22nd Street, 6th Floor, New York, NY 10010; 212-352-3019.

page 44
ROUND STOOL with green legs from David Stypmann, see above. MARTHA STEWART EVERYDAY COLORS PAINT in "Garden Glove Green" (C13), available at Kmart, see above. PINE CONSOLE, $2,700, from Mariette Himes Gomez Associates, 506 East 74th Street, New York, NY 10021; 212-288-6856. AFRICAN STOOL, $150, from Cobweb, 116 West Houston Street, New York, NY 10012; 212-505-1558.

page 45
MARTHA STEWART EVERYDAY COLORS PAINT in high-gloss "Daisy White" (H26) on scroll-legged table, and "Goat's Beard" (E14) on straight-leg stool, available at Kmart, see above. Custom GLASS TABLETOP from Glaaass, see above. French CHROME LAMP, $700, from Troy, 138 Greene Street, New York, NY 10012; 212-941-4777. STEREO from Harvey Electronics; 800-254-7836 for store locations. Black-and-white PHOTOGRAPH by Maria Robledo, 212-406-3211. Custom FRAME from Chelsea Frames, 207 Eighth Avenue, New York, NY 10011; 212-807-8957. Blue Tiffin glass VASE, $150, from David Stypmann, see above. "Fine Madagascar" GRASS CLOTH on straight-leg stool, $63 per yard, from Hinson & Company, 979 Third Avenue, New York, NY 10022; 212-688-5538. To the trade only.

page 47
Wooden PORCH-POST LAMPS, $275 for pair; LAMPSHADE covered in 1940s wallpaper, $36; small PAINTED STAND, $65; from Ruby Beets Antiques, see above. CHAIR COVER sewn by Ann Baderian; 718-359-0309. Karthika YELLOW-STRIPED FABRIC (#33004/41D) from Clarence House, 211 East 58th Street, New York, NY 10022; 212-752-2890. To the trade

only. BENJAMIN MOORE FLOOR PAINTS in "Chamois" (#200), "Putty" (#235), and "Bryant Gold" (#HC7), see above. COTTON SHEETS, $80 for fitted and flat in queen; PILLOW SHAMS, $50 each; and GLASS DECANTER, $80; all from Calvin Klein Home, see above. 1960s satellite GLOBE LAMP, $300, from Bilhuber, see above. Alvar Aalto NESTING TABLES, $1,010 for set of three; STACK STOOL (#60), $145; and SLATTED BENCH, $485; all from ICF Group, see above. LINEN SHEETS, double/queen size (#0302), $445 per set; LINEN PILLOWCASES, standard size (#0302), $145 per pair; BOX-STITCH DOWN COMFORTER, double/queen size (#0705), $350; Zurich DOWN PILLOW, standard size (#0406), $65; Monaco DOWN PILLOW, Continental size (#0402), $130; all from Garnet Hill; 800-622-6216. Free catalog. BED SKIRT sewn by Ann Baderian, see above.

page 48
Glass VASE, $66, from L. Becker Flowers, 217 East 83rd Street, New York, NY 10028; 212-439-6001. Low ROUND STOOL, $2,400, from Mariette Himes Gomez Associates, see above. "Limerick" PLUM UPHOLSTERY with KHAKI TRIM, $23.95 per yard, by Waverly; 800-423-5881 for store locations. GRAY CORD, 98¢ per yard, from M&J Trimmings, 1008 Sixth Avenue, New York, NY 10018; 212-391-9072. Nickel-plated articulated SWING-ARM LAMP, $695, from James Hepner, 130 East 82nd Street, New York, NY 10028; 212-737-4470. BEDSIDE CLOCK, $50, from Ad Hoc, see above. Fiberglass DESK LAMP by David Weeks, $220, from Shì, 233 Elizabeth Street, New York, NY 10012; 212-334-4330. 4'-by-6' Samarkand KILIM RUG (#1944), $255; COTTON BLANKET (#0537), $155 for twin size; Wamsutta PILLOWCASE (#0230), $42 per pair for king

size; twin FLAT SHEET (#0230), $26; and twin FITTED SHEET (#0231), $18; all from Garnet Hill, see above.

page 49
1950s VANITY STOOL, from Historical Materialism, 125 Crosby Street, New York, NY 10012; 212-431-3424. MARTHA STEWART EVERYDAY Egyptian cotton TOWEL and WASHCLOTH, available at Kmart, see above. BUTTONS, 39¢ each, from M&J Trimmings, see above. CERAMIC TRAY; 30"-by-48" RUG; GLASS BOTTLE with metal cap; and GLASS CANISTERS; all from Ad Hoc, see above.

LAMPS & SHADES

pages 52 to 67
Assorted lamp-making supplies: LAMPSHADE FRAMES are available from: The Lamp Shop, P.O. Box 3606, 130C Hall Street, Concord, NH 03302-3606; 603-224-1603. Mainely Shades, 100 Gray Road, Falmouth, ME 04105; 800-624-6359. Toolex, 418 Route 31N, Ringoes, NJ 08551; 609-466-3096. Victorian Classics, 4128 NE Sandy Boulevard, Portland, OR 97212; 503-282-7055. Aro Wire, 2122 Arron Street, Los Angeles, CA 90026; 213-389-2391. DeWire, 128 N. Broadway, Lovelaceville, KY 42035; 502-876-7586. Paramount Wires, 4110 W. Chicago Avenue, Chicago, IL 60651; 773-252-5636. PRESSURE-SENSITIVE SELF-ADHESIVE STYRENE, $14.30 per yard, from The Lamp Shop, P.O. Box 3606, Concord, NH 03302-3606; 603-224-1603. Catalog $3. Also available from Service Fabrication Corp., 1935 Fairfield Avenue, Chicago, IL 60647; 815-356-6101. YARDSTICK COMPASS, $6, and HEAVYWEIGHT PAPER, $3 to $10 per sheet, from New York Central Art Supply, 62 Third Avenue, New York, NY 10003; 212-473-7705. 18"-by-24" self-healing CUTTING MAT, $42.50,

and Sobo CRAFT GLUE, $2 for 4 ounces, both from A.I. Friedman, 44 West 18th Street, New York, NY 10011; 212-243-9000. $15 minimum order. ¼" Filmoplast T BOOKBINDING TAPE, $12.45 for 33' roll, and 7" BONE FOLDER, $4, from Talas, 568 Broadway, Suite 107, New York, NY 10012; 212-219-0770. Catalog $5. ⅛" HOLE PUNCH (#312-9509), $8.40, from Sax Arts & Crafts, P.O. Box 51710, New Berlin, WI 53151; 800-558-6696. Catalog $5.

pages 52 and 60
WOOD VENEERS, $27.50 to $200 per sheet, from Constantine's, 2050 Eastchester Road, Bronx, NY 10461; 718-792-1600 or 800-223-8087. Free catalog.

pages 53 and 54
Red LAMP BASE, $150, from David Stypmann Co., 192 Sixth Avenue, New York, NY 10013; 212-226-5717.

page 55
Teak-and-alabaster LAMP BASE from AERO, 132 Spring Street, New York, NY 10012; 212-966-4700.

pages 58, 59, and 61
27"-by-39½" heavyweight "Whatman Creswick" VINTAGE PAPER, $35 per sheet; 27½"-by-39¼" ELEPHANT-HIDE PAPER, $2.55 per sheet; and 22"-by-30" "St. Armand" SLATE-BLUE PAPER, $6.30 per sheet, from New York Central Art Supply, see above. SATIN CORD (#2 Rattail), 60¢ per yard, and ⅛" ULTRASUEDE LACING, 98¢ per yard, both available from M&J Trimming, 1008 Sixth Avenue, New York, NY 10018; 212-391-9072.

page 59
Green vase LAMP BASE from David Stypmann Co., see above.

pages 62 and 63
SATIN CORD, 60¢ per yard, from M&J Trimming, see above. RAFFIA available from florists and craft stores.

page 67
SMALL LAMPSHADE by Shades from the Midnight Sun/S. Wellott Co., 66 Boulder Trail, Bronxville, NY 10708; 914-779-7237.

SHELVES

page 70
"AGRA" RUG, $45,000, from Galerie Shabab, 112 Madison Avenue, New York, NY 10016; 212-725-5444. SLIPPER CHAIR, $2,100, from Bilhuber, 330 East 59th Street, New York, NY 10022; 212-308-4888. White ART POTTERY, $40 to $295 per piece, from LEO Design, 413 Bleecker Street, New York, NY 10014; 212-929-8466. COFFEE TABLE, $695, from Lars Bolander, 5 Toilsome Lane, East Hampton, NY 11937; 516-329-3400. Glass-topped SIDE TABLE, $2,100 for three nesting tables, from Mariette Himes Gomez Associates, 506 East 74th Street, New York, NY 10021; 212-288-6856. 1700s BALUSTER LAMP, from Pierre Deux Antiques, 369 Bleecker Street, New York, NY 10014; 212-243-7740.

page 71
1¾" wood CORBEL BRACKETS, $20 each, from Mad River Woodworks, P.O. Box 1067, Blue Lake, CA 95525; 707-668-5671 or 800-446-6580. Catalog $3. FERN PRINTS from Treillage, 418 East 75th Street, New York, NY 10021; 212-535-2288.

page 73
6'-by-9' Lhasa CARAVAN RUG, $3,295, and walnut Eames STOOL, $800, from ABC Carpet & Home, 888 Broadway, New York, NY 10003; 212-473-3000. Chinese ELM TRUNK, $550, from Coconut Company, 131 Greene Street, New York, NY 10012; 212-539-1940. CUSTOM SHELVING by Eric Walton/Icon Design Studio, 338 West 49th Street, New York, NY 10019; 212-581-

8529. T.H. Robsjohn-Gibbings CHAIR and OTTOMAN, $3,200 for both, from Donzella, 17 White Street, New York, NY 10013; 212-965-8919.

page 74
SHAKER PEGS, $15.20 for 50, from Shaker Workshops, P.O Box 8001, Ashburnham, MA 01430; 800-840-9121. Free catalog. MARTHA STEWART ARAUCANA COLORS PAINT on wall in "Putty," $75 for 2½ liters, from Fine Paints of Europe, Box 419, Woodstock, VT 05091; 800-332-1556.

page 75
CUSTOM SHELVING by Wood Design, Inc., 158 Kenwood Avenue, Fairfield, CT 06430; 203-254-3176. STORAGE BOXES, $100 each, from Eric Walton/Icon Design Studio, see above. 1930s SCROLL-ARMED SOFA from AERO, 132 Spring Street, New York, NY 10012; 212-966-1500. VINTAGE LINEN on pillow from Paula Rubenstein Limited, 65 Prince Street, New York, NY 10012; 212-966-8954. Eames ROUND TABLE, $375, from Regeneration, 38 Renwick Street, New York, NY 10013; 212-741-2102. Arne Jacobsen STACKING CHAIR, $350, from ICF, 305 East 63rd Street, New York, NY 10021; 212-750-0900. Heath CERAMIC BOWL, $62, from Galileo, 37 Seventh Avenue, New York, NY 10011; 212-243-1629. VASE, from Mxyplyzyk, 125 Greenwich Avenue, New York, NY 10014; 212-989-4300. PORTRAITS of children and feet courtesy of Victor Schrager. Custom METAL FRAME on feet photograph from Bark Frameworks, 85 Grand Street, New York, NY 10013; 212-431-9080. By appointment only. PHOTOGRAPH of umbrellas by William Abranowicz for Takashimaya.

page 76
Linen HEMSTITCH NAPKINS by Sferra, $13.50, from Ad Hoc, 410 West Broadway, New York, NY 10012; 212-925-2652. Aluminum

I-BEAMS, $16.50 per foot, from Space Surplus Metals, 325 Church Street, New York, NY 10013; 212-966-4358.

page 77
SHELF SUPPORTS (#63Z06.04), $5.50 for 20, from Lee Valley Tools, P.O. Box 1780, Ogdensburg, NY 13669; 800-871-8158. Catalog $5. STAINLESS-STEEL SHELF, $150, from M. Kabram & Sons, 257 Bowery, New York, NY 10002; 212-477-1480.

pages 78 and 79
CUSTOM SHELVING by Wood Design, Inc., see above. Fabric WINDOW SHADES, $47 each, from East End Installations, Inc., 412 Main Street, Center Moriches, NY 11934; 516-878-9000 or 800-287-4554. X-BACK CHAIR, $1,650, from Mariette Himes Gomez Associates, see above. Polka-dot VASE, $125, from Rooms & Gardens, 290 Lafayette Street, New York, NY 10012; 212-431-1297. Large glass HURRICANE, $290, from Coconut Company, see above. Antique THROW PILLOWS, $85 to $225, and VINTAGE FABRIC on window seat, from Paula Rubenstein Limited, see above. PRESSED BOTANICALS, $450, from Treillage, see above.

page 82
Alto DEMILUNE TABLE, $600, from ICF, see above. MARTHA STEWART ARAUCANA COLORS PAINT on shelves in "Drabware," $75 for 2½ liters, from Fine Paints of Europe, see above.

page 83
CUSTOM SHELVES by George Christiansen/Pequot Remodeling Corporation, 140 Towne House Road, Fairfield, CT 06430; 203-259-3390. MARTHA STEWART ARAUCANA COLORS PAINT on shelves in "Silkie White," $75 for 2½ liters, from Fine Paints of Europe, see above. COTTON VELVET, $19.95 per yard, from B&J Fabrics, 263 West 40th Street, New York, NY 10018; 212-354-8150.

page 84
Full-size BED KIT, $440 to $550, from Shaker Workshops, see above. MARTHA STEWART ARAUCANA COLORS PAINT on wall in "Putty," $75 for 2½ liters, from Fine Paints of Europe, see above.

page 85
Circa-1880 CHAIR by E.W. Godwin, $1,000, from Marc O. Rabun, 115 Crosby Street, New York, NY 10012; 212-226-5053. IRON BRACKETS, $100 per pair, from Mxyplyzyk, see above. 52" PAINTER'S LINEN (#2325) on shelves, $20.50 per yard, from Pearl Paint, 308 Canal Street, New York, NY 10013; 212-431-7932. Alabaster BOWLS from Treillage, see above. Black VASE, $160, from Rooms & Gardens, see above.

page 87
Woven LINEN BOOK TAPE, $5.95 for 10 yards, from Talas, 568 Broadway, New York, NY 10012; 212-219-0770

page 88
Custom SHADOW BOXES available from Eric Walton/Icon Design Studio, see above.

page 89
MARTHA STEWART EVERYDAY COLORS PAINT in "Potato Peel" (F14), available at Kmart; 800-866-0086 for store locations. PRATT & LAMBERT PAINT in "Mineral Red" (#1874); 800-289-7728 for nearest retailer. Circa 1810 DRABWARE and JASPERWARE platters and plates, $3,200 for set of 12 plates and 4 platters, from James II Galleries, 11 East 57th Street, 4th floor, New York, NY 10022; 212-355-7040. Louis XVI-style OPEN ARMCHAIR from John Rosselli, Ltd., 255 East 72nd Street, New York, NY 10021; 212-737-2252. To the trade only. Fretwork VASE and Japanned Queen Anne SIDE CHAIR from J. Garvin Mecking Antiques, Inc., 72 East 11th Street, New York, NY 10003; 212-677-4316.

SCREENS & MIRRORS

page 90
Custom LEADED GLASS by L.A. Feldman from Stained Glass Design and Restoration, 373 Broadway, New York, NY 10013; 212-925-8246. CHROME-PLATED HINGES, $10 to $48 each, from Kraft, 306 East 61st Street, New York, NY 10021; 212-838-2214. BENJAMIN MOORE ENAMEL PAINT in "Linen" on folding screen; call 800-826-2623 for nearest retailer.

page 91
Custom wooden FRAMES (#cosc), $20 to $40 each, from Graphik Dimensions; 800-221-0262. Bronze CANDLEHOLDERS, $45 and $52, from Troy Antiques, 138 Greene Street, New York, NY 10012; 212-941-4777. Glass CANDLEHOLDERS, $35 to $50, from David Stypmann Co., 192 Sixth Avenue, New York, NY 10013; 212-226-5717. Louis XV MARBLE-TOP TABLE, $5,600, from Rooms & Gardens, 290 Lafayette Street, New York, NY 10012; 212-431-1297. ORNAMENTAL HINGES (#64PC), $1.10 each, from Simon's Hardware & Bath, 421 Third Avenue, New York, NY 10016; 212-532-9220.

page 93
Heavy-weight CANVAS STRETCHERS, $3.97 to $46.17 per pair, and LINEN FABRIC, $10.64 to $77.97 per yard, from Pearl Paint, 308 Canal Street, New York, NY 10013; 212-431-7932. 1¼" stainless-steel DOUBLE-ACTION HINGES, $16.95 per pair, from Simon's Hardware & Bath, see above. 1¼" cream TWILL TAPE, $1.59 per yard, from M&J Trimmings, 1008 Sixth Avenue, New York, NY 10018; 212-391-9072. FRAMED PHOTOGRAPH, "Parlor Mantle with Flare Vases," by John Dugdale, $2,200, from Wessel+O'Connor Gallery, 242 West 26th Street, New York, NY 10001; 212-242-8811.

pages 94 to 97
Custom SCREEN FRAME KIT from Kestrel Manufacturing, 9 East Race Street, Stowe, PA 19464; 610-326-6697 or 800-494-4321. Free catalog. ⅛" PASTEL-GREEN GLASS, $3.75 per square foot, by Wiss, from S.A. Bendheim, 122 Hudson Street, New York, NY 10013; 212-226-6370. BENJAMIN MOORE ENAMEL PAINT in "White Dove," see above. WHITE LINEN, $21.95 per yard, from B&J Fabrics, 263 West 40th Street, New York, NY 10018; 212-354-8150. Brass BARREL FITTING, $2.50 per pair, and ROD, $3 per foot, from BZI Distributors, 105 Eldridge Street, New York, NY 10002; 212-966-6690. Double-action BRASS HINGES, $2.49, from Simon's Hardware & Bath, see above. MARTHA STEWART ARAUCANA COLORS PAINT, $75 for 2½ liters, from Fine Paints of Europe, Box 419, Woodstock, VT 05091; 800-332-1556.

page 98
Nickel-plated BRASS HINGES, $2.49, from Simon's Hardware & Bath, see above. No. 3 GROMMETS, $30 per box, from BZI Distributors, see above. 1¼" STEM CASTERS, $4.69 for four, by Shepherd Products, available from Home Depot, Builder's Square, Ace Hardware, and TrueValue stores.

page 99
Nineteenth-century French PARLOR CHAIR with striped upholstery fabric from Coconut Company, 131 Greene Street, New York, NY 10012; 212-539-1940. MARTHA STEWART ARAUCANA COLORS PAINT in "Oceana," $75 for 2½ liters, from Fine Paints of Europe, see above. ⅛" CORK, $20.19 per 8' roll, from Janovic Plaza, 215 Seventh Avenue, New York, NY 10011; 212-645-5454. 12" LINEN LAMPSHADE, $29, from Oriental Lampshade

Company, 223 West 79th Street, New York, NY 10024; 212-873-0812. TOPOGRAPHICAL MAPS (7.5 minute series), $4 per sheet, from the U.S. Geological Survey Information Services, Box 25286 D.F.C., Denver, CO 80225; 303-202-4700 or 800-435-7627.

pages 102 to 109
Custom MIRRORS from Zecca Mirror & Glass, 617 West 48th Street, New York, NY 10036; 212-957-4297.

page 102
COTTON RUNNER, $13.75 per square foot, from Woodard & Greenstein American Antiques, 506 East 74th Street, New York, NY 10021; 212-988-2906.

page 103
BUCKRAM FABRIC, $8.50 per yard, from Talas, 568 Broadway, Suite 107, New York, NY 10012; 212-219-0770. 30"-by-40" FOAM BOARD (#14-7172), $4.29 per sheet, from Charrette Corp., 127 East Street, New Haven, CT 06511; 203-624-5000. GIN BOTTLE, $70, from Troy Antiques, see above.

page 106
2" SATIN RIBBON, $13.50 per yard, from Hyman Hendler & Sons, 67 West 38th Street, New York, NY 10018; 212-840-8393. RIBBON MIRROR, $89, from Martha By Mail; 800-950-7130.

pages 107 to 109
MIRROR FRAME, $147, from Kestrel Manufacturing, see above. BEADED TRIM (#11261), $3.30 per foot, and COMPOSITION MEDALLIONS (#7373F), $4.62 each, from the Decorator's Supply Corporation, 3610-12 South Morgan Street, Chicago, IL 60609; 773-847-6300. Custom ANTIQUED MIRROR from Rosen Paramount Glass, 45 East 20th Street, New York, NY 10003; 212-532-0820. Antique SIGN LETTER from Woodard & Greenstein American Antiques, see above.

PILLOWS & THROWS

page 110

ANTIQUE TICKING, $65 to $225 per piece, from Paula Rubenstein Limited, 65 Spring Street, New York, NY 10013; 212-966-8954. Printed LINEN FABRICS, $140 per yard, from Bennison Fabrics, 76 Greene Street, New York, NY 10012; 212-941-1212. CASHMERE THROW, $495, from ABC Carpet & Home, 888 Broadway, New York, NY 10003; 212-473-3000. RATTAN FURNITURE, $1,200 to $7,000, from the American Wing, Main Street, Bridgehampton, NY 11932; 516-537-3319. MARBLE LAMP, $450, from Rooms & Gardens, 290 Lafayette Street, New York, NY 10012; 212-431-1297. Terre mélange EGG; circa-1825 English OAK CHAIR; antique Belgian MIRRORED SCONCES; large ENGLISH BASKET; BAMBOO SIDE TABLE; eighteenth-century CHINESE TABLE; circa-1800 INLAID BOX; vintage GARDEN BOOKS; and MARBLE PLATE; all from Mecox Gardens, 257 County Road 39A, Southampton, NY 11968; 516-287-5015. SHOE BOXES, $18 each, and HAT BOX, $16, from Bell'occhio, 8 Brady Street, San Francisco, CA 94103; 415-864-4048. No catalog available.

page 111

1900 French PETIT ARMCHAIR from Coconut Company, 131 Greene Street, New York, NY 10012; 212-539-1940.

pages 112 to 135

Custom-made FEATHER-AND-DOWN PILLOWS from Allied Down, 84 Oak Street, Brooklyn, NY 11222; 718-389-5454.

page 113

"Spinnaker" TUXEDO SOFA from Crate & Barrel; 888-249-4155 for store locations. Paul McCobb COFFEE TABLE from AERO, 132 Spring Street, New York, NY 10012; 212-966-1500. 1950s Robsjohn-Gibbings TRIPOD FLOOR LAMP, $1,800, from

Donzella, 17 White Street, New York, NY 10013; 212-965-8919.

page 116

"Potomac" LAWSON SOFA from Crate & Barrel, see above. Handmade Tibetan unibeige RUG from Odegard, 200 Lexington Avenue, Suite 1206, New York, NY 10016; 212-545-0069. To the trade only. BASKET-WEAVE TRIM (#P-0102-2), $46.50 per yard, from Rogers & Goffigon, Ltd., 979 Third Avenue, Suite 1717, New York, NY 10022; 212-888-3242. To the trade only.

page 117

"Knihult" BRIDGEWATER SOFA from IKEA; 410-931-8940 for East Coast locations; 818-912-1119 for West Coast. Antique RATTAN COFFEE TABLE, $460, from English Country Antiques, Snake Hollow Road, Bridgehampton, NY 11932; 516-537-0606.

page 117 and 121

MONOGRAMS from Penn & Fletcher, 242 West 30th Street, New York, NY 10001; 212-239-6868.

page 122

"Knihult" BRIDGEWATER SOFA from IKEA, see above. Leaf-patterned JACQUARD (#C96017) from Decorator's Walk, 979 Third Avenue, New York, NY 10022; 212-319-7100. To the trade only. VELVET TRIM, $5 to $6 per yard, from Hyman Hendler & Sons, 67 West 38th Street, New York, NY 10018; 212-840-8393. WICKER TRUNK, $425 for two, from Coconut Company, see above. Deco German blond wood NESTING TABLES from AERO, see above. Louis XVI beech-wood FAUTEUIL, $6,200, from James Hepner Antiques, 130 East 82nd Street, New York, NY 10028; 212-737-4470. Handmade Tibetan CHAKKU RUG from Odegard, see above.

page 124

"Celery" GREEN LINEN (RL1704-27) from Decorator's Walk, see above. "Allegro" STRIPED LINEN,

$20 per yard, from the Silk Trading Co., 360 South LaBrea Avenue, Los Angeles, CA 90036; 213-954-9280. "Pandora River" GREEN LINEN, "Pandora Maize" YELLOW LINEN, and "Summer Place Popsicle" LINEN, $48 to $81 per yard, from Rogers & Goffigon, Ltd., see above.

page 125

"Spinnaker" TUXEDO SOFA from Crate & Barrel, see above. TICKING FABRICS, $44 to $55 per yard, and WICKER CHAIR, $690, from Coconut Company, see above. CAMEL-TICKING PILLOW, $125, from Laura Fisher Antiques, 1050 Second Avenue, Gallery #84, New York, NY 10022; 212-838-2596. Linen HAND TOWEL used to make button pillow, $25, from Ad Hoc, 410 West Broadway, New York, NY 10012; 212-925-2652. TOWELING, $30 per yard, from Paula Rubenstein Limited, see above.

page 130

COLORED LINEN, $20 to $30 per yard, from B&J Fabrics, 263 West 40th Street, New York, NY 10018; 212-354-8150. "Borax" COUNTRY LINEN (#92504-02) on headboard, $100.50 per yard, from Rogers & Goffigon, Ltd., see above. "Natural" LINEN TAPE, $2 per yard, from Bell'occhio, see above. "Natural" LINEN (#302) on small pillow, $36 per yard, from Mecox Gardens, see above. HEADBOARD from John Rosselli International, 523 East 73rd Street, New York, NY 10021; 212-772-2137. To the trade only. Antique French BISTRO TABLE, $1,200, from Rooms & Gardens, see above. Chrome SWING LAMP, $850, from Wyeth, 151 Franklin Street, New York, NY 10013; 212-925-5278. Antique PICTURE FRAME with nineteenth-century TULIP DRAWING from Paula Rubenstein Limited, see above.

page 131

"Orchid" PINK LINEN, $21.95 per yard, and BEIGE AND LAVENDER

LINEN, $20 to $30 per yard, from B&J Fabrics, see above. GOLD LINEN (#RL1704-1), $10 per yard, from Decorator's Walk, see above. "Pistachio" GREEN LINEN, $10 per yard, from Trebor Fabrics, 215 West 40th Street, New York, NY 10018; 212-221-1610. Small ALARM CLOCK from Ad Hoc, see above. Antique FISH DRAWINGS from Paula Rubenstein, see above.

page 133

BUCKSHOT CORD, $1 per yard, from BZI Distributors, 105 Eldridge Street, New York, NY 10002; 212-966-6690.

page 134

BURNT-ORANGE CASHMERE WOOL, $44.95 per yard, from New York Elegant Fabrics, 240 West 40th Street, New York, NY 10018; 212-302-4980. DUSTY-PURPLE and GRAY CASHMERE, both used as trim, $150 per yard; WHITE WOOL CASHMERE, $95 per yard; all from Weller Fabrics, 24 West 57th Street, New York, NY 10019; 212-247-3790. LIME-GREEN DOUBLE-FACE WOOL, $49.95 per yard, and BUTTER-YELLOW WOOL, $49.95 per yard, both from B&J Fabrics, see above. 1½"-wide CORNFLOWER-BLUE DOUBLE-FACE RIBBON used as trim, $3 per yard; 2"-wide YELLOW DOUBLE-FACE RIBBON used as trim, $4 per yard; 3"-wide RUST-ORANGE DOUBLE-FACE SATIN RIBBON, $4 per yard; from Hyman Hendler & Sons, see above. LAVENDER WOOL FLANNEL, $34 per yard, from Beckenstein Men's Fabrics, Inc., 121 Orchard Street, New York, NY 10002; 212-475-6666.

page 135

Supercale white cotton PILLOW-CASE by Wamsutta, $24 per pair, from ABC Carpet & Home, 888 Broadway, New York, NY 10003; 212-473-3000. BLANKET sewn by Gayle Dragt, 240 East 6th Street, Apt. 1, New York, NY 10003; 212-254-0829.

Picture Credits

PHOTOGRAPHY

William Abranowicz
front cover, pages 4, 5, 6, 10, 11, 12, 13, 15 (top left, bottom left and right), 16, 17, 18, 19, 20, 21, 22, 23 (top and bottom), 26, 27, 28, 29, 36 (top), 39, 46 (right), 47 (top left, bottom left), 70, 87, 88, 89, 90, 92, 93, 94, 95, 96, 97, 98, 99, 100, 101, 124, 127, 130, 131, 132, 134, 135, back cover (middle row, second from left)

Fernando Bengoechea
pages 68, 69

Henry Bourne
pages 110, 111

Jim Cooper
pages 112, 113, 114, 116, 117, 118, 119, 120, 121, 122, 123, 125, 129, back cover (bottom left)

Carlton Davis
pages 66 (top), 67 (left)

Reed Davis
pages 66 (bottom row), 67 (right)

Todd Eberle
pages 91, 102, 103, 104, 105, 106, 107 (top left and right, bottom left), 108, back cover (middle row, right)

Thibault Jeanson
pages 3, 14, 15 (top right), 23 (right), 36 (bottom), 37 (left), 38, 40, 41, 42, 43, 47 (top right), 52, 53, 54, 55, 56, 57, 58, 59, 60, 61, 62, 63, 71, 72, 73, 74, 75, 76, 77, 78, 79, 80, 81, 82, 83, 84 (right), 85, 86, back cover (middle row, left; middle row, third from left)

Stephen Lewis
pages 48 (right), 51 (left), 84 (left), 107 (bottom right), 109

Victoria Pearson
page 2

Victor Schrager
page 64

Matthew Septimus
page 32

Simon Watson
pages 8, 24, 25, 30, 31, 33, 34, 35, 37 (right), 44, 45, 46 (left), 48 (left), 49, 50, 51 (right), back cover (top; bottom right)

ILLUSTRATIONS

Harry Bates
pages 65, 115, 118, 119, 120, 121, 126, 128, 129, 132, 133

Index

If you have enjoyed this book,
please join us as a subscriber
to MARTHA STEWART LIVING
magazine. The annual subscrip-
tion rate is $26 for ten issues.
Call toll-free 800-999-6518,
or visit our Web site,
www.marthastewart.com.